The Enrolled Agent Tax Consulting Practice Guide

Learn How to Develop, Market, and Operate a Profitable Tax and IRS Representation Practice

Author: C. Pinheiro, EA ABA®
Editor: Cynthia Sherwood

PassKey Publications
Elk Grove, CA

Dedication

This book is dedicated to all of the financial professionals who contributed their expert opinions to make this book such a success.

Thank You:
Owen Arnoff, EA
Chet Burgess, EA
Darrell Carp, EA
Kristin Delfau, EA
Bill Fulcher, EA MBA
David Hatt, EA MS
Dineen Huft
Gabrielle Fontaine, PB
Gary W. Lundgren, EA

Full Disclosure

All of the Enrolled Agents mentioned in this book are real individuals. None of the EAs received any compensation for being interviewed for the book. The author has no financial interest in and receives no compensation from the businesses or organizations mentioned in this book.

In the case studies and other examples, the clients' names have been changed to protect the privacy of the individuals.

Other Books by PassKey Publications

How to Start a Successful Home-Based Freelance Bookkeeping and Tax Preparation Business

The Chef's Commandments:
Maximize Your Kitchen's Profitability:
Building and Maintaining a Successful, Profit-Driven Restaurant

PassKey EA Exam Review
Individuals, Businesses and Representation
IRS Enrolled Agent Exam Study Guide

ISBN 13: 978-09822660-4-5
www.PassKeyPublications.com

Edited by Cynthia Sherwood, ***www.secondsetofeyes.com***.

Table of Contents

Foreword

By Kristin Delfau, EA MA

Author of: ***Turbo-Mom's Guide to Saving Money Without Wasting Time***

One of the more entertaining moments I had when becoming an Enrolled Agent happened in the Prometric testing room: I was waiting to be called in with a dozen other people, most of them CPA candidates. The test administrator came out and said, "IRS test?" while looking at me—and promptly everyone, especially the CPAs, scooted their chairs away from mine.

Becoming an Enrolled Agent is truly special—it is not a course of study in college or something that you just "do." Rather, it is a designation sought out by tax practitioners who truly care about their clients—and their own professionalism—in order to gain knowledge and credibility in an increasingly complex and rapidly changing field.

Becoming an EA is only half the battle—then what do you do with yourself and your designation? *The Enrolled Agent Tax Consulting Practice Guide* is an excellent, step-by-step approach to building your own practice. Unlike many other guides written about starting your own (insert generic adjective here) business, Christy's book focuses on the specific needs of the tax preparation community. With solid and detailed advice on everything from how to configure your office space to how to market your practice, she makes it easy to understand the components of a successful practice. Her personal experiences—

both good and bad—are excellent learning tools to accompany her recommendations.

I especially enjoyed her chapter on choosing your clients wisely, which in the long term is much more profitable and much less stressful. It goes against the traditional approach to building a business, which is "take everyone who walks in the door and when you are profitable enough, weed out the bad ones later." Eventually, the "bad" clients cost you so much time and billable hours that you do not have the energy to find more "good" clients. She emphasizes a great point: to help your clients and stay in business, you need to get paid—and *on time!*

Christy also delves into other areas of generating revenue for your practice. From S-Corp work to representation at audit, she takes a hands-on approach from how to set your fees to what to expect in the process. She is also one of the few authors to emphasize Errors & Omissions Insurance, which is essential in *any* tax practice, even if you are doing only twenty-five returns per year. The cost of coverage is reasonable and worth it in case you ever have to use it.

For Enrolled Agents, particularly sole practitioners, one of the toughest facets of the business can be marketing. We don't like to think of ourselves as "in sales" and thus, often figure if we "hang out a shingle," the clients will find us. Unfortunately, there is too much competition out there for that approach to work!

Instead, *The Enrolled Agent Tax Consulting Practice Guide* provides six helpful chapters on how to market your practice effectively and without going bankrupt doing so. I liked that Christy addressed the importance of niche marketing—we cannot possibly be experts in every facet of tax law, and that's okay. It's also reasonable to refer clients to others who specialize in fields of tax law that are not your forte. You will build credibility within the profession and perhaps receive some referrals in return!

I am thrilled that Christy wrote this book to help both new and seasoned EAs build and grow their practices. Though it is relatively easy to locate continuing education and tax update classes online and around the country, it is rare to find a practical and well-written book on tax practice management. Christy Pinheiro has now written the book that I searched for years ago when starting my own firm—so use it to your advantage and go build your tax practice!

Introduction

Welcome to the first nationally-distributed tax consulting guide designed *specifically* for Enrolled Agents! I've met lots of tax professionals through the years. I've also worked as an accountant in multiple tax practices, two CPA firms, and one government agency. I feel that the main reason why most tax pros fail to strike out on their own is because they do not believe they can generate the client base that will give them the income stream of a regular full-time job.

This book is designed to help you develop and market your financial services to the public. The main issue that EAs face is how to grow and promote their practices. In talking with tax professionals, their questions are always the same:

"How do I build up my client base?"
"How can I avoid deadbeat clients?"
"How do I fire a bad client?"
"Are engagement letters really necessary?"
"How do I encourage more client referrals?"
"How much should I charge for services?"

This book offers real answers to all of these questions. Read multiple interviews with established, highly profitable EAs. You will hear from *them* how they keep their practices in the black and keep clients (and money) rolling in. If you have the tax knowledge and a desire to succeed in this business, this book will help you realize your dreams.

Experienced EAs can offer valuable insights to help you succeed in your own practice. Enrolled Agents spend most of their billable hours doing three things: tax consulting, tax compliance, and representation. All of these services are inter-connected, but they are not the same.

1. Tax consulting occurs *before* the imposition of tax. This is also called *tax planning*. Most tax professionals do some amount of tax planning for their clients since it is the best opportunity to save clients money. Tax consulting is a great way to offer your clients a valuable service and also generate billable hours throughout the year.

2. Tax compliance is also commonly known as tax reporting. The preparation of tax returns falls under this umbrella. EAs prepare tax returns and build their core practice on tax return preparation. Tax compliance occurs *after* the imposition of tax. In most cases, when you are preparing a client's tax return, it is already too late to advise the client on how to reduce his/her tax burden. Some exceptions to this rule include retirement plan contributions, which can be done after year-end.

3. Representation is the last stage in the tax planning process. Representation occurs when a taxpayer's return (or other reporting) comes under attack by the IRS. Enrolled Agents are uniquely qualified to represent taxpayers, because they are the only federally-authorized tax professionals.

Many EAs genuinely enjoy representation, and have built entire practices upon serving the needs of these clients. IRS audits, OIC[1] submissions, and formal IRS Appeals all fall under the "representation umbrella." In order to represent a client, you generally must submit a signed Power of Attorney to the IRS (**Form 2848**).

This book assumes that you are already an Enrolled Agent, or that you are a tax practitioner planning to take the EA exam at a future date. Some of the information, such as the chapter on audit representation, will only apply to someone who is enrolled to practice before the IRS—a great privilege that we, as Enrolled Agents, share with CPAs and tax attorneys.

You may have just passed the EA exam, or you might be an experienced Enrolled Agent looking for tips on how to build your practice and make it more profitable. Either way, this book has something for you.

Chapter 1

The Wide World of Tax Consulting

"It's tax time. I know this because I'm staring at documents that make no sense to me, no matter how many beers I drink."

-Author Dave Barry

Tax Consulting is Big Business

Independent tax consulting is one of the best businesses in the world. You sell a high-end product that most people cannot live without—namely, tax preparation. Enrolled Agents offer other financial services as well, such as bookkeeping, payroll, IRS representation, tax planning, and so on. The possibilities are endless.

When you become an EA, you also have the luxury of choosing a part-time business or working year-round. You can work during tax season, or decide to offer year-round financial services. Many EAs are retired accountants or former IRS agents who now run highly profitable individual tax practices.

According to Paul Edwards, the *Self-Employment Expert*, a tax preparation business is one of the best home-based businesses to start in the United States.[2] EAs are tax specialists, so their greatest profit potential is in their ability to target a niche market. Edwards states in his book that the EA exam is the best path to becoming a successful, licensed tax preparer:

The more lucrative alternative is to become a licensed tax preparer known as an ***Enrolled Agent****. The EA designation is the only one granted by the federal government… The EA is entitled to appear before the IRS at hearings to represent clients. EAs may prepare taxes for individuals, corporations, partnerships, estates, trusts, and any entities with tax reporting requirements.*

–Paul Edwards, *The Self-Employment Expert*

If you enjoy finance, a tax consulting business may be just the right option for you. As taxes grow more confusing and the IRS gets more aggressive with its enforcement, taxpayers are looking for professionals who can prepare their tax returns and also represent them in the event of an audit.

Some believe that accountants will someday become obsolete. They say that computer software or "the flat tax" will make tax accountants unnecessary. The fact of the matter is that the idea of a "flat tax" has been around for decades. And computer software, like TurboTax® or TaxCut®, can only do so much. In fact, most tax professionals report that a big part of their business comes from amending self-prepared returns that taxpayers have messed up trying to prepare themselves.

There are twenty million businesses in the United States alone; all of them need some type of financial guidance. Even in bad economic times, there are many opportunities for EAs to find clients. Tax planning, bookkeeping, payroll, and consulting are just some of the services EAs may offer.

Options for Starting a Tax Practice

At the beginning, you will have to consider how to start your tax practice. You can purchase a franchise or an existing tax practice. You can also decide to "go solo" and strike out without doing either.

1. Going Solo: This is the most difficult route, but also the least expensive. If you already do tax returns for family and friends, consider a quick marketing blitz to those people. Ask them to refer their friends to you. Place classified ads on Craigslist and other sites, and visit local businesses and let them know you are available for their bookkeeping and tax preparation needs. Walking into local businesses in-person seems to work the best.

Going solo might be the hardest way to start, but if you have the capital to grow organically, or if you have a second income that helps support your lifestyle while you grow, it may be the best way to go. You won't have any legal obligations to a franchiser, and you won't have the financial burden of purchasing another tax practice. If you decide to go this route, estimate at least five years to build up your client base.

2. Buying a Franchise: Buying a tax franchise, like *H&R Block* or *Jackson Hewitt*, is an easy way to have instant name recognition. A franchise is a legal arrangement where the franchisee (you) agrees to pay a fee for the legal right to use the franchiser's business name or trademark. In most cases, the franchise fee is ongoing, meaning that you must pay a portion of your profits to the franchiser year after year.

Franchises have a better opportunity for success the first year they are in business, mainly because of name recognition. But owning a franchise is costly. You must consider all the costs associated with the franchise before you purchase. You will likely be required to pay franchise fees, royalty payments, and advertising fees to the franchiser.

You may also have significant restrictions on how you run your business. And you may be restricted on where you can actually open your business.

3. Buying an Existing Tax Practice: You may want to consider purchasing an existing tax practice. Tax businesses that have been in existence for at least five to ten years have a better profit potential and higher customer loyalty. If you purchase a tax practice that is in an existing location, consider the location of the practice.

How is the foot traffic? Is there ample parking? What does the neighborhood look like? Is the building in disrepair? Has the area taken an economic downturn lately? All of these questions are important to consider if you are going to purchase a tax practice "in place."

Check the average age of the clients. If all the clients seem to be over fifty, this may be a practice that is not growing. A successful practice has a good mix of age groups, business types, and income levels.

Find out why the seller is relinquishing the practice. Is it because of illness, death, or retirement? It is very important that you understand why the practice is being sold. The last thing you want is to purchase a practice from someone who was disbarred or is currently under review for ethics violations.

Look at the last five years of financial statements and tax returns. Examine the client listing, and count how many clients are return customers. The real value of any practice is in customer loyalty. A high turnover in the client base might signal a situation where the practice has serious issues.

Make sure that you get advice from local professionals and lawyers and bankers. Ask how the practitioner is viewed in the community. If the practice's reputation is not good, find out why.

Does the purchase include hardware, software, and staff? Purchasing a practice outright is a serious investment in both time and money. Make sure that you can handle all of the complicated tax returns before you purchase another practice. Be realistic about your skills; if you don't have a lot of corporate experience, do you really want to purchase a tax practice that is 50 percent corporate work?

All of these questions must be answered fully before attempting to purchase a tax practice. It is probably a good idea to use a formal intermediary, such as an attorney or a broker who specializes in the sale of accounting firms.

Tax Consulting: Advantages

There are definite **advantages** to tax consulting, such as:

1. Enrolled Agents provide a product that almost everyone needs, namely, tax preparation and audit representation. People need help understanding tax law more than ever, because Congress has made tax law so convoluted. Add in complexity of state taxation, and it is a wonder that anyone attempts to self-prepare his own return.

2. It is easy to flesh out an existing tax practice with ancillary financial services. You can add bookkeeping, payroll, tax planning, representation, business valuation, as well as other profitable services. It is easy to build a year-round tax practice. You can also opt to work part-time, just during tax season. Financial services offer some of the best flexibility of any profession.

3. Tax consulting is extremely lucrative. Most EAs charge $100 an hour (or more) for services. Although not all of your time is going to be billable time, you can still earn a very good living doing tax consulting. If you specialize, you can earn even more. Corporate taxation, partnerships, and estate tax returns are tax specialties that can generate huge revenues.

Self-employed Enrolled Agents earn salaries of about $49,000-$116,000 per year, on average. [3] Over 25 percent of tax practices in the United States gross more than $150,000 a year.[4] This amount goes up for practices that offer more financial services. Enrolled Agents who are also Enrolled Actuaries make substantially more than those who are not. The amount that you can earn also varies considerably by location and years of experience.

Tax Consulting: Disadvantages

Of course, along with advantages come *disadvantages.* Here are some disadvantages to tax consulting:

1. Your work cannot be relegated to an unskilled employee. You are required to sign the returns, speak with the IRS, and do most other sensitive tasks yourself.

2. If you get sick and cannot work, your income flow stops. You need to work hard at the beginning until you have enough revenue to be able to hire an assistant or receptionist. You can mitigate this issue by working with a partner, or having employees who are either licensed or have good tax training.

3. Dishonest clients are risky because they may put you in a situation where you (unknowingly) file a false return, and bring the wrath of the IRS's *Office of Professional Responsibility* upon your head. Although you may be able to defend your decisions, it's harder if you do not regularly use engagement letters. Trust your gut instinct about which clients are more trouble than they are *worth*! You are always going to have some risk from unscrupulous clients.

4. Tax law is extremely complex and getting more intricate every year. It takes a sharp mind to be able to keep up with the constant changes. You must be dedicated to continuing education. Every year, you must learn tax law changes. There are no shortcuts.

There are risks and rewards in every business. You can make a very nice income as a self-employed Enrolled Agent as long as you have the client numbers and billable hours to support your practice. The first step is to get those clients in the door. The rest is up to you. Now let's cover some basics.

Home Office or Commercial Location?

At the beginning, your finances dictate your office location. A tax preparation business can be started from home with a personal computer and a good tax software program.

Approximately 38 percent of tax preparers work from a home office. The number of tax preparers who practice out of a "brick and mortar" business location is 63 percent.[5]

Most Enrolled Agents *start out* either:

1. Working from home with a home-based tax practice or
2. Working for another tax practitioner, such as an EA or a CPA, to gain valuable experience before striking out on their own.

Some EAs are part-time preparers, and generally work out of their home. I've met a number of part-time EAs that do about 50-100 tax returns each season, working out of their home. Often, these EAs also work regular full-time jobs, and prepare tax returns after work and on weekends.

If you do decide to work out of a home office, you need to set firm boundaries. Create a business atmosphere in your home office. Clearly define your workspace, and do not allow your personal home life to mix. Your office should be isolated from family gathering places—away from the living room or kitchen.

Use a separate telephone line for your business. Make sure there is some type of barrier to your office. It can be a door, a temporary partition, or even a hanging drape.

You must make sure that your home office has a basic work area. Make sure there is room for a desk or table and your computer. You should purchase a filing cabinet to store taxpayer files. You will probably purchase paper by the case, and you will need a place to store other office essentials. You should have a cabinet or closet to hold office supplies.

Even if you decide to "go paperless," you still have to hold onto some original documents. This is especially true if you offer other services. Notary services and insurance services are two examples where you are required to hold on to original documents.

Even if you don't meet with clients in your home, you need to set aside a special place just for your work. Make sure your home office is clean, organized, and free of clutter. Get a pretty plant or a nicely-framed print. If your home office is full of books, toys, or exercise equipment, it is harder to concentrate on your business. Clean up your workspace, and try to avoid distractions. This will allow you to stay more focused even in a home office setting.

Purchase a paper shredder to properly dispose of any documents that include confidential information, such as bank statements or credit card bills. In fact, make sure that your entire home office is secure. Consider investing in an alarm system. Security companies (like ADT or Broadview Security) charge as little as $30 a month; it is an investment in your safety and well worth the money.

There are some serious drawbacks to working out of your home. Are you prepared to accept strangers into your home? If this is a concern, you may want to do all of your consulting at the *client's location*. The National Association of Tax Professionals reports that 2 percent of tax preparers work only in the client's location. Many freelance bookkeepers also work exclusively at a client's business.

Working from a Home Office—Drawbacks

1. Lack of Privacy. If you live in a small apartment or have children at home, you may feel that a home office is not private enough. Pets, family interruptions, and home life may interfere with your ability to work effectively.

2. Managing Children and Pets. How will you manage your children when you are working from home? If they are in school, you can work during those times. Managing your pets might be difficult, too. Many people are allergic to dogs and cats; what happens if your client comes over and starts sneezing uncontrollably? Some people are deathly afraid of dogs. What if your dog starts barking while you are on the phone? Keep pets outside, or away from your office altogether. Try to anticipate problems in advance.

3. Lack of Security. Are you comfortable bringing strangers into your home? Do you feel unsafe allowing clients inside your private residence? This is especially important if you are female. If you're uncomfortable allowing clients into your home, offer to do initial interviews elsewhere. If the client has a business, do the interview there.

4. Professional Image. Are you sure your home office is appropriate for client meetings? Is your house cluttered, dirty, or smelly? If you feel that your home office is not professional enough, consider investing in a virtual office (covered later).

5. Local Restrictions. Sometimes, local zoning laws will not allow you to run a business from your home. Make sure that you verify that you can run your business from your home. It goes without saying that most of the time you will need to purchase a business license in order to run your business, even if you are just working from home.

The Virtual Office

A virtual office is an inexpensive solution to a common problem. Virtual offices usually start at about $100 a month. The virtual office allows users to have a prestigious mailing address at a fraction of the cost. Basically, virtual offices allow you to have a business *address* and partial use of an office. They are professionally staffed.

One of the biggest benefits of a virtual office is the use of a receptionist. The receptionist is trained to answer your dedicated line with your business name. This is included in the cost of your office lease. The calls are routed to voicemail, or forwarded to another phone number.

This is a huge benefit for very little cost. No payroll, no health benefits, and the receptionist can sign for packages and other deliveries. It's a very nice option for those who have a little money and cannot afford a permanent commercial location. If you have a virtual office or home office, you will have to do most of your promotion on the Internet or in other ways.

Usually, you get a business phone line, a shared receptionist, voicemail, and a business address. Most of the time, you are granted the use of shared meeting rooms or other office space. The offices are leased for "on-demand" use. Virtual office users do not lease space full-time.

The most frequent virtual office users are accountants and attorneys. In a poor economy, the use of virtual offices actually goes up. As accountants give up their commercial business offices to save money, they are looking for an inexpensive (and yet professional) solution.

Virtual offices are available in every major city. You can check Craigslist, the Yellow Pages, or your local newspaper. All of them should have advertisements for virtual offices in your area.

Virtual Office Testimonial

Our business is a start-up company. We can't afford to commit ourselves to a traditional lease. We chose to lease a virtual office instead. We prefer the flexibility of being able to hire meeting rooms only when we need them. We use the phone, voicemail, and mail forwarding services. It's been a very cost-effective solution for us.

A Permanent Office Location

Once you become successful enough, you can break out and get a permanent office. A stable office location is important to your success, and it shows a level of professionalism that a home office does not. Most Enrolled Agents agree that working out of an office gives them more flexibility. EAs generally charge more when they work at an office.

The location of your business will impact your billable rate. The better your location, the better your clientele. The location of your permanent office is an extremely important decision. Ask yourself about the type of client you want to attract. Location is the most important factor.

Is your hometown the most lucrative location for your tax practice? Consider a tax practice outside of your own hometown. All too often, beginners are attracted by a cheap commercial location, only to find that the clientele is subpar, nonexistent, or low income. Do not be wooed by a beautiful office location with little marketing potential, either. A gorgeous office in an obscure location is not a good choice. A pleasant office in a well-traveled area is the best bet.

A tax practice in a low-income neighborhood will encourage more EIC (Earned Income Credit) tax returns and you will probably have to offer RALs (refund anticipation loans). Tax practices in poorer areas do better if they offer RALs. There is also a higher risk of EIC fraud.

An office on a busy street encourages more walk-ins. An office in a professional building will encourage more upscale business clients, but fewer walk-in clients. Check out your neighbors. Look for banks, insurance agents, law firms, architectural firms, and other professional service companies. These are the type of businesses that attract high-end clients.

Study the demographics of your location. Target your specific market. Look at age, housing, profession, and economic status. Your local Chamber of Commerce should be able to help you. Do some serious research before you choose your permanent location.

Your office should be convenient for your clients. Always make sure there is plenty of parking. Nothing infuriates a client more than having to circle the block ten times looking for a parking spot. Then they arrive late for their appointment, and it's an inconvenience for you, too.

The physical condition of your office will also impact client perceptions. Make sure your office is in a modern building, or at least one that has functioning electrical, plumbing, and restroom facilities.

Do you plan to expand? Does the office have extra space? Perhaps you plan on hiring a bookkeeper soon. Take this into account when you choose your office. You need to make sure you have space for a receptionist or bookkeeper (or both) if you plan on hiring within twelve to twenty-four months.

Your office should have, at a minimum, a workspace for you, storage space for client files, a waiting area for clients, and an assembly area that will allow you to compile returns. You can use movable partitions, such as cubicle walls, to break up the space. Try to plan at least three years in advance. Make sure your office can accommodate a growing practice, if that is what you want.

Does your office have signage? Is your office visible from the street? Is your office inside a professional building? Is there potential for you to pick up business clients within the building? Make sure there is not another tax accountant already working in the same location.

If you have signage that is visible from the street, make sure your sign is crisp, easy to read, and without peeling letters or paint.

Make sure you have a coat rack, or another convenient place for people to put their belongings. Have coffee, bottled water, and tea available. Consider purchasing snacks during your busiest time; offer them to your clients as they arrive. Make sure your bathroom is sparkling clean with plenty of supplies. This includes a packet of tampons and sanitary napkins.

You may want to purchase a small package of diapers and baby wipes if you serve a lot of families. These small touches are very inexpensive, but make a big difference. Clients notice. We will cover more about office decor later.

In a while, you will read interviews with other Enrolled Agents who took the plunge and opened up their own practices from scratch. This takes a lot of hard work and long hours, but it is possible to succeed by just going out there and setting up your own practice.

The US Tax System

Most taxpayers believe that the IRS decides tax law, but actually it is Congress that writes and passes tax law. The IRS is charged with enforcement and interpretation of tax law.

The US Courts also "interpret" tax law in the course of regular litigation. The courts are not bound by *Revenue Rulings* or *Revenue Procedures*, and both of these are frequently challenged by taxpayers (and their attorneys) who believe that the IRS has misinterpreted Congress's *intent.* Enrolled Agents are bound by Circular 230 to uphold the tax laws of the United States. However, this does *not* mean that you must strictly follow IRS publications.

As we all know, there are many interpretations of current tax law. Your responsibilities as a tax professional include keeping up-to-date on current case law. Following tax court decisions can help you represent your clients, and may help you be more aggressive, while still staying within the law. Every Enrolled Agent knows that the US Tax Court is more favorable to the taxpayer than the IRS. This is why so many cases end up in tax court every year.

Tax professionals agree that the current poor economy has forced the IRS to step up collection efforts. Although IRS employees are, for the most part, fair and reasonable, every tax professional has at least one anecdote of an IRS auditor who was ignorant, rude, or overbearing (or all three!).

William V. Roth, Jr., a former US senator, co-authored *The Power to Destroy*, a scathing book about IRS collection practices. The book is full of taxpayers who have been driven to the brink of financial ruin by overly aggressive collection activities. There are even stories of taxpayers who committed suicide because of the IRS.

> "The IRS has extraordinary collection powers. There is no other agency of government that has the power to collect debt, or to sell property prior to a judicial proceeding." [6]
>
> **Jerome Kurtz, former IRS Commissioner**

Studies show that average Americans are terrified of the IRS, sometimes with good reason. We know that the IRS targets low income and middle income taxpayers unequally.[7] The IRS disproportionately targets tax returns showing the Earned Income Credit (EIC). In 2002, one out of every forty-seven low-income taxpayers was audited. For taxpayers making over $100,000 a year, only one out of every 145 was audited.

And more recently, the audit rates for those with incomes over $1 million fell to 5.6 percent in 2008 from 6.8 percent in 2007. The overall number of millionaires audited declined from 23,200 to 21,874, even though the actual number of millionaires went up.[8]

Although the IRS does not explain how or why it chooses a certain segment of the population for audits, some tax professionals believe there is a more sinister motive. Some believe that the lower classes are being targeted because they are the least likely to be able to afford representation.

Every tax professional knows that taxpayers who represent themselves during an examination are treated differently than taxpayers who have competent representation. Since most audit cases cost at least a few thousand dollars, low income and middle income taxpayers will usually try to represent themselves.

Unfortunately, by the time tax professionals get involved, usually the audit case is beyond repair. In the end, a great deal of our job is simply damage control.

Regardless of the situation, you must be prepared to represent your client to the *best of your ability*. The best protection taxpayers have against the IRS is for their representatives to be well-informed about current tax law.

Many of us have won audit cases simply on technicalities. A good friend of mine, a CPA working out of Sacramento, told me about a case where the IRS auditor let the audit deadline expire. The CPA won the audit case simply because the auditor forgot about the case and let the statute expire (this is called *"blowing the statute"* in IRS circles).

Many EAs specialize in IRS audit representation. Some are even former IRS employees who know a great deal about how the IRS functions on the "inside." These former IRS agents go on to form highly lucrative tax consulting firms of their own. You will hear from one former revenue officer, Darrell M. Carp, EA, later on in this book.

Ten Skills Required for Tax Consulting

1. You Must Have Good Tax Preparation Skills.

We all have to start somewhere, but don't try to break out on your own until you have good knowledge of taxation. If you can't figure out how to prepare a long form (**Form 1040**) by hand, you should probably wait a few years before your start your own tax practice.

This may seem obvious, but basic skills are required in order to start a tax business. You must be able to do taxes accurately and reliably. You can't make a $50,000 mistake your first year—it could put you out of business before you even start! Take the time to get the experience you need by working for another preparer, or working for a financial company where you get exposed to tax law.

If you offer tax preparation, bookkeeping services, or payroll services, you need to remain up-to-date on changing tax law and reporting requirements.

The positive side of this is that you don't need any type of degree; all you need is some experience or a few tax courses to get started. Most tax preparers start out by taking a class. Beginner's tax courses are offered by most of the major tax franchises as well as most junior colleges. You can also choose to take a home study course. The Universal Accounting Institute[9] has a well-respected online program. The benefit of a home study course is that it is easier for working people to accommodate their existing schedules.

Private courses can also teach you how to start your own practice, which other courses may not. This is especially true of the tax courses offered by H&R Block and other franchises. That is because the main goal of the franchise tax courses is to train potential new employees for the coming season.

However, if you want to gain valuable experience working with the public, you still may want to consider taking the H&R Block or Jackson Hewitt course. If you do well, you will be invited to work for them during the tax season. This is how many tax preparers get their start.

In addition to your regular continuing education requirements for the EA license, you will need to remain up-to-date on your state's payroll laws. You may want to offer sales tax return preparation, as well. In that case, you would have to stay current on requirements for your state and locality. Continuing education comes with the territory.

Professional certification impresses clients and allows you to charge a premium for services. People expect to spend more for someone who has a professional certification. Even if you do not have a college degree, post your enrollment certificate in a nice frame on your wall. (Don't be cheap! Use professional framing—clients *will* notice!)

Clients are awed by appearances (sometimes even more than by substance!) It makes a big difference when clients see that you have a certification. Of course, if you have a college degree, post that, too. I also post my membership certificates to the NATP and NAEA.

2. You Must Have Basic Money Management Skills.
This may seem obvious, but the reason why many EAs fail their first few years is because they *over*estimate their profits and *under*estimate their costs. You need to understand how to track costs and manage the money you make.

Track your spending and expenses carefully (with good bookkeeping software, such as QuickBooks or Peachtree). Watch your cash flow. In the beginning, focus on producing income and be conservative with purchases.

Make sure that you bill clients and collect payment in a timely manner. When clients are slow to pay, look for new clients to replace them. You're in business, too—don't forget that your services are valuable and should be treated as such. Your tax practice is not a charity. If a new client comes in and wants you to perform services without a retainer, look out! You may be throwing your valuable billable hours down the toilet.

3. You Must Have Self-Discipline.

Since you are self-employed, it's great that you won't have a boss breathing down your neck. But for some people, this is actually a bad thing! In order to be successful in a freelance business, you need motivation to work, promote yourself every day, and stick to a schedule.

Not all of your time will be billable time, especially at the beginning. You should spend at least 15 to 20 percent of your time marketing your services and finding new leads.

4. You Must be Able to Market Yourself.

Some people find self-promotion distasteful. If you do, get over it—*quick!* The success of your tax practice is dependent on how well you market yourself to the public. Take a deep breath. Get over your shyness or any fear you have of meeting new people. This is a very customer-service oriented business, and the sooner you learn how to market yourself to the community, the better.

5. You Must Have Basic Computer Skills.

These days, it's impossible to do business as a tax preparer without basic computer skills. EAs prepare tax returns on computers using tax software. Most of your bookkeeping clients will use QuickBooks. Consider becoming a QuickBooks ProAdvisor (more about this program later), because it will often generate referrals that turn into tax clients.

Most of your small business clients are going to expect a clean tax return and computer-generated reports. Take the time to become proficient in basic word processing and how to use the Internet.

6. Learn How to Manage Interruptions.
Everyone who owns a business has to manage interruptions. Some of these are beyond your control. Even in the most organized business setting, about 10 percent of the interruptions are important enough that you have to stop work in order to attend to the problem.

Practice reducing the remaining interruptions. Use voicemail, and don't answer your cell phone every time a client calls. If the matter is important, he or she will leave a message. Devise a standard for what qualifies as a reasonable interruption. Ask yourself—"is this really worth stopping my billable hours?" If you have a list of important clients, perhaps you can just answer inquiries from those few. The list should be short, and the number of interruptions should be infrequent and important.

7. You Must Have a Good Work/Life Balance.
If you have the strong desire to work for yourself and be your own boss, you can do it! But don't kill yourself at the office at the expense of your family and friends. Everyone knows that business gets tough during tax season, but even then, take at least one day a week to relax, spend time with family, and catch up on personal tasks. If you don't, "burn-out" will soon follow, and you will find yourself making mistakes.

Take care of yourself even more so during your busiest times, because your health, sanity, and the quality of your work product will be affected by how well you balance your work and home life.

8. You Must Have Good Communication Skills.
This is a *people* business. Develop a friendly attitude. Learn how to explain things to clients in a way that makes it easy for them to understand. Your clients may not understand tax law, but they

will appreciate it when you explain WHY they have to pay so much money to the IRS.

Communication skills may determine your eventual level of success. Many consulting firms believe that the ability to communicate is even more important than technical skill![10] So, by the same token—you may be the smartest, most experienced tax professional in your area, but if your closest competitor is warm and friendly and you're *not*, you will be losing clients to the competition!

9. Learn How to Approach People.

In order to be successful in your own business, you must get over your shyness. You have to learn how to sell yourself assertively. At the beginning, you can do everything that employees might do when looking for a job. Make appointments with local business owners and "interview" with them. Locate companies that you'd like to work with, and introduce yourself. Attend trade association meetings in the fields for which you specialize. Shake lots of hands.

To land the client that you want, offer a sample of your work (like a sample financial statement). Show them your outstanding work ethic and your superior skills. Dress professionally at all times. This means no jeans, no torn clothing, no ratty shoes, or stained shirts. Even if you don't have a lot of money, you can always purchase nice professional clothing at a local thrift store. There's no excuse for dressing inappropriately when you are trying to portray yourself as an accounting professional.

10. You Must be *Enrolled to Practice* Before the IRS!

Unenrolled preparers cannot accept IRS representation cases. Only Enrolled Agents, CPAs, and attorneys have the privilege to represent taxpayers before the IRS. That is because only EAs, CPAs, and attorneys are *enrolled to practice* before the IRS.

An unenrolled preparer may not represent taxpayers before the IRS (except in extremely limited circumstances). And if an unenrolled preparer *falsely claims* to be an Enrolled Agent, he or she is committing a felony. There are numerous instances where this has happened.

A recent case involved an unenrolled preparer[11] in Fairfield, California. He was arrested for falsely claiming to be an Enrolled Agent. He stands accused of falsely presenting himself as an IRS Enrolled Agent.

For this, he faces **sixteen felony charges**. The IRS caught him because he actually submitted **Form 2848** for clients and claimed that he was an EA *on the Power of Attorney*. This is such a serious offense that it usually garners jail time.

For *falsely* claiming to be an EA

The maximum penalty for each false statement is five years in prison, a $250,000 fine, and a three-year term of supervised release. For misuse of the IRS name, the maximum penalty is one year in prison, a $100,000 fine, and a one-year term of supervised release.

So you see, so many people *want* to be Enrolled Agents that they actually *lie* about it! Now, don't you feel proud that you are an EA? You should be!

Chapter 2

Help! I'm a Beginner!

"Tax preparers can earn thousands of dollars during tax season. But they must know how to do the job, advertise, professionally present themselves, and establish their fee schedule."

-**Robbi Erickson,** Newspaper Columnist

Office Basics for the Beginner

The following chapter is advice for the true beginner. If you already have a bustling practice, this might be a little remedial for you. You may want to skip to the next section, where we cover many ways to expand your existing tax practice.

Choosing a name for your practice

If you are a beginner, you will need to choose a name for your business. Make sure that your practice name clearly reflects the type of work that you do. Do *not* use a humorous name, such as ***Achy-Breaky Taxes*** or ***IRS Blasters.*** This will come off as unprofessional.

Make sure you do a web search to figure out if your business name is already taken on the Internet. See if your business name is available as a domain (website address) right now. You can check website availability simply by going to a website registration provider like *Register.com* or *Go Daddy.com* and typing in the name you want to use.

The availability of the domain name may be a big part of choosing your company name. Maybe you want to name your company "Tax Pro Central," but you find out that the domain, *www.TaxProCentral.com* (website address), is already taken. Someone is already using the perfect name that YOU picked out! The nerve!

So you have to choose another name. In doing a domain name search, you find out that *www.SuperiorTaxes.com* is available. Perfect. You purchase the domain and you're on your way.

Perhaps you simply want to do business under your own legal name. That's fine too. Lots of accounting firms are named after their founders or managing partners. When you purchase your website domain, you might not find an exact match, especially if your name is a common one. Try different variations. For example, if your name is Paula Jones, EA, try the following:

www.PaulaJonesEA.com
www.PJTaxes.com
www.PaulasTaxService.com
www.JonesTaxConsulting.com
www.JonesTaxService.com
www.PJonesTaxes.com
www.JonesTaxes.com

You get the picture. Most EAs start out with a simple website, and graduate to a full-blown site from there.

A side note: If you can't get a website address (domain name) ending in ".com" or ".net," then move on and think of something else. All the other domain addresses, such as ".info" or ".biz," are not suitable if you are trying to maximize your Internet search potential. Play around with different website addresses. You'll eventually find one that you like.

Once you decide on a name, you may want to officially trademark it. You may want to invest in a trademark attorney in order to trademark your name and logo. A good trademark attorney will do a search for you, and let you know if a similar name is already in use. If you use an attorney, the trademark filing will cost you about $500-$800 including the cost of government fees.

I attempted to trademark my business name my first year. I found out that the name was rejected by the United States Patent and Trademark Office (USPTO). Too bad—I had already purchased my business cards, stationery, and website domain. In the end, I used a trademark attorney to sort out the mess. I wound up paying for the rejected application and for an entirely new application because my first business name was not accepted (someone else had already trademarked something similar).

A good attorney will also do a thorough search and let you know if a similar trademark is already in use. For me, it was worth it. I just don't have the time or the expertise to deal with legal matters, and I thought the cost was reasonable.

You can also search the Internet for a trademarking service—some companies will fill out the paperwork for a fee. Shop around and see what you can afford.

Get Professional Stationery

You're in business—let's make it official. Even if you are working from home, you should avoid an amateur image. Many new Enrolled Agents neglect this part of their business. Don't give your clients the impression that your business is unprofessional. You don't need to spend a lot of money. You just need to pay attention to the details. Clients notice. I always notice when someone hands me a cheap business card printed on an inkjet printer. I think to myself—this guy is small potatoes. He's not really serious about his business.

Don't use photocopied brochures or stationery. Quality paper stock is inexpensive if you buy in bulk. Use at least 24-pound paper for your letterhead. Your envelopes should match. Make sure all of your business correspondence is typed and all your promotional material looks professional. You can use a software program specifically designed for this. *Microsoft's Print Shop* is one example, and it costs less than $50.

Nice business cards and letterhead indicates professionalism. It shows that you are serious about your profession. Investing in your image from the very beginning is the first step in your success. You don't need to buy very much, especially at the beginning, but you should make a small investment in fine paper and business cards.

Once you've **got** someone as a client, then feel free to switch to cheaper paper to send out invoices. But when you introduce yourself to potential clients, make sure that you put your best foot forward. This means having nice business cards printed on fine paper.

You can purchase fine paper and print your own stationery using a home printer (laser printers work better than inkjet printers). This is probably the cheapest option and can cost less than $10 for about fifty sheets. It also allows you to print only as much as you need. Fine envelopes and resume paper can make excellent professional stationery if you take the time to design and print them yourself.

Your correspondence is like a miniature advertisement for your business. If you have a good eye, you can use the templates provided by online stationery suppliers, such as *www.VistaPrint.com*, at very reasonable prices. When ordering your business cards, consider purchasing cards with a photograph of yourself.

People are less likely to throw away business cards with a photograph on them. This is why real estate agents use photographs on their business cards. If you decide to use a photographic business card, use a nice photo.

Portrait studios in Walmart charge less than $20 for a nice, professional-looking photograph. You can also have a friend take a photo of you at the office, perhaps in front of your (clean) desk. Dress professionally for your photograph. You will likely use the same photo for your website and other promotional material, such as your brochures. Don't use an outdated photo from high school or your wedding. It looks slapdash and unprofessional.

Once you get your business cards, hand them out everywhere you go: in restaurants, at mixers, and to relatives and friends. Include a business card with every invoice. Business cards are cheap, and you never know when one of your clients is going to hand your card to a friend.

Invest in a Separate Phone Number

A separate telephone number is required, even if you work from home. It can be a cellular phone, landline, or VOIP line. You can get an additional line installed at your home for about $100. Most home-based tax preparers use a second telephone line.

There will come a time when you will probably want to get another line, possibly for a fax. I used my home telephone number to receive faxes the first two years, and then I finally had a separate fax line installed. If you have a permanent office, the rates will vary based on your carrier.

Perhaps you are working from home, and you don't have the money or inclination to invest in a second landline (if, for example, you rent an apartment and your landlord won't allow you to install an additional line). You can buy an inexpensive, pre-paid cellular phone for about $20, and just pay as you use it. This option is best for home-based tax preparers and bookkeepers who are just starting out.

Tracfone is the most popular pre-paid cell phone provider in America and for good reason—it's the cheapest and its coverage is good.

I used a Tracfone my first year and I was happy with the coverage and the price. A pre-paid cellular phone is the easiest way to get a separate phone line without spending a fortune or making a long-term commitment. If you rarely use the cell phone, it will only cost you about $10 a month to maintain service.

You can use this inexpensive cell phone as your "business line," and post the number on your website. This helps add credibility to your new company, and it shows that you plan to be around for a while. If you choose to keep specific business hours, you won't have to answer the phone at a time when you are "off duty."

Separate phone numbers can be added to your existing home landline with *Distinctive Ring* service from your phone company. It is, however, important for your contacts or clients to have a reliable means to contact you.

If you use a voicemail service, do not record anything "funny" or personal. Your message should always begin by giving the name of your business. Ask callers to leave their name and telephone number. Then add that you will return calls as soon as possible. You may want to mention your office address and your business hours. Keep it simple.

Telephone Etiquette

Telephone etiquette is extremely important. Always be courteous and professional when you answer your business line. Here are some telephone pointers:

1. Answer by the second ring.
During your normal business hours, you should answer the phone by the second ring if possible. During the busy season, if you have decided to limit your phone interruptions, make sure you have voicemail or an answering machine.

2. Set firm call-back times.
Set strict times for when you will return phone calls, such as 11 a.m. or 2 p.m. This will help you manage your time, and keep you from eating up all your billable hours on the phone.

3. Keep kids away from your phone line.
Do not let your children answer your business phone number! In fact, it's a good idea to keep family members (who are not employees) from answering your business telephone.

4. Return calls promptly.
Always try to return client calls within twenty-four hours. Even if you don't have an answer right away, let them know you are researching their question.

5. Prioritize your best clients.
Answer calls from your best clients first. As many of us know, sometimes the worst client is the one that won't stop bothering you. If you are being harassed by a deadbeat client, offer to set up a "telephone consultation" and let them know there will be a fee for your time, payable in advance. This will usually take care of the problem, because deadbeat clients use phone calls to get free advice.

6. Quiet in the background!

Make sure that all of your telephone conversations are free of background noise. Your client should not hear dogs, children, or music in the background. This is especially true when you are speaking with a client for whom English is a second language because it makes it harder for them to understand you, and vice versa. If you cannot avoid background noise, it is better to let your caller go to voicemail. Call the client back when you have quiet time.

7. Do not leave callers on hold for long periods.

If you must, let them know you are on another call. Take their name and number, and let them know you will call them back right away.

8. Be prepared for every call.

When you return a client's call, try to have the client's file in front of you. Don't make a lot of small talk, and make sure you allow the client to explain his situation fully.

9. Identify yourself first.

When you answer the phone, don't just say "hello." Make sure you clearly identify yourself, or state the name of your business. Develop a short script. You'll get used to it in no time.

10. Protect yourself! Always take notes.

Always! This is especially true during your busy times, when you are less likely to remember individual conversations. A great habit to start is to include a lined sheet of paper in the client file. Use this sheet to record client conversations. Many tax professionals have been saved from court proceedings simply by having good records.

Sample Phone Message Script

Thank you for calling *Tallon's Tax Service.* Our office hours are Monday through Friday, 10 a.m. to 7 p.m., and on Saturdays by appointment only. If you have reached this message during our normal business hours, we are currently helping other callers. Your message is important to us.

Please leave your name and telephone number, and we will return your call within twenty-four hours.

Buying Tax Software

This is *the tough question.* Professional tax software is expensive. Your software will probably be your biggest expense. High-end tax software is usually more expensive than your computer. The first year that I purchased Lacerte, I remember being shocked that the software cost $500 more than my laptop.

Purchase the best software you can afford. It is difficult to switch software later. In fact, it is more difficult to switch software at a later date than it is to choose software the first time you are starting out.

Good software reduces your man-hours. In this respect, a good software program "pays for itself." Your tax software should meet your business needs and make your job easier overall.

Let your finances be your guide. Just remember, there's nothing wrong with the pay-as-you-go method (such as the pay-per-return feature offered by Lacerte and Ultra Tax). If you decide to use this feature, you will be charged a one-time fee for software. Then, each time you process a tax return, you will be charged a fee *per use.* If you have fewer than 100 clients, this is usually more cost-effective. If you have *more* than 100 clients, it is better to purchase the full license for unlimited use. Crunch the numbers yourself and figure out which method is best for you.

According to NATP's latest tax software survey, the most popular *professional* tax software is as follows:

Tax Software	% Using
ATX	11%
Drake	24%
Lacerte	13%
Ultra Tax	9%
ProSeries	20%
TaxWise	8%
Other	15%

The prices of each software suite vary wildly, and many of them offer price-breaks to first-time buyers or tax preparers who are switching software programs. Lacerte, ProSeries, and QuickBooks are all owned by Intuit.

I use Lacerte, and when I first signed up, I paid for the full license and they offered me free copies of the previous five years of their software program. This was a nice perk because I had quite a few clients who had back-tax issues. The program paid for itself the first year. Call around and ask what each company has to offer. Then make your choices based on what you feel is best for your business. Don't use price as your only deciding factor. Ease of use should be high on your list.

If you are already a member of NATP, log in to their "members only" area and read NATP's yearly tax software survey. For the last twenty-three years, NATP has gathered information about competing software products and compiled the information into a report for their members.[12] The NATP report gives you great information about all the different types of tax software out there, including price, services offered, and how to contact each company for information about their tax products. Once again, this is worth the price of membership to NATP, one of the best professional organizations out there.

Office Equipment and Furniture

Remember, your tax business is supposed to support you, not the other way around. Think in terms of how long it will take for each new piece of equipment or software to pay for itself. If you purchase used equipment, you can save a lot of money. Here's a short review list of what is "bare bones" in order to get started:

- Recent version of Microsoft Office, QuickBooks, and a good *professional* tax software suite (examples: Lacerte, ATX, ProSeries).
- Desktop computer or laptop with a cable, DSL, or Wi-Fi connection
- Inkjet or laser printer
- Separate telephone number with voicemail or an answering machine
- Box of CDs and a couple of reams of copy paper
- Business cards and stationery
- A back-up device, such as a USB drive or external back-up drive
- Postage scale and/or postage meter

A few of the above items need some brief explanation. Your computer doesn't have to be cutting edge, but don't use a relic either. You will probably be required to use a PC computer, rather than a MAC (Macintosh), because most tax software platforms only run on PCs. I currently use a custom-designed Sony laptop for all my tax preparation and writing needs. It goes everywhere with me.

Laptops are more expensive, but they are portable. If you plan to work from home, a virtual office, or go to client locations, a laptop is a better choice. If you have a permanent office location, you may prefer a desktop computer. Desktop computers are less expensive, and will suit your needs if you plan to expand.

Make sure you understand what's involved if you decide to upgrade to a new computer. I sadly discovered that my older versions of Lacerte would not run on Vista, (Microsoft's operating system after XP). At the time of this printing, Microsoft has already released Windows 7, which is bound to add even more software compliance issues into the mix.

In the end, I had a custom computer designed specifically for me, running Microsoft's XP, which is an older operating system. This allowed me to have newer computer hardware, but still use my older software programs. I serve quite a few delinquent filers every year, and I like being able to access older versions of Lacerte right on my desktop.

A fast Internet connection (**NOT** dial-up) is a **must** because e-mail and e-file have become vital in this field. In fact, 99 percent of all tax offices offer e-filing to their customers. In some states such as California, e-filing is mandatory.

A high-end printer is not as vital as it used to be since much of your work will be delivered via e-file, upload, e-mail, CD, or flash drive. But some clients and tax preparers like to see tax returns in hard copy as well. Even while some offices go paperless, they will still need a printer for some things, such as Power of Attorney forms and other forms that require a client's wet signature. If you plan to print out a hard copy of every single one of your returns, you will need to invest in a high-volume printer. Numerous companies offer all-in-one printers. These all-in-one printers also work reasonably well as scanners and photocopiers.

My printer is an all-in-one laser printer, and it cost $400. It uses a toner cartridge and a drum, rather than individual ink cartridges. I save money in the long run because the toner cartridge has a cheaper cost-per-copy. I still have a small back-up printer that I use for emergencies. You can purchase a cheap inkjet printer for less than $40.

If you plan to work in a paperless environment, an inexpensive printer might be all that you need. But if you start to do a lot of printing, the ink will become a huge expense. Individual ink cartridges are expensive. It might be a good idea to invest in a good printer from the start. If you have more than one tax preparer in your office, it is a good idea for everyone to have his or her own dedicated printer. This solves many problems as you get closer to the April deadline.

Don't even think about submitting a handwritten tax return, anywhere, EVER. Don't give handwritten tax returns to clients. Don't file handwritten returns with the IRS. No one wants to slog through your handwritten scribble, and the risk of errors on a handwritten tax return is exponentially higher than a tax return that is printed or e-filed.

A word about software: Buy a legal copy of all software, including Microsoft Office. DO NOT borrow a friend's copy and use it in your business. Not only is this illegal, but it will be disastrous if something happens to your software while you are working on a deadline.

If you own the software, often a simple reinstall will solve the problems caused by an unexpected power outage or other issues that can mysteriously corrupt files at the most crucial moment. Many preparers remember the Intuit *e-file crash of 2007*, when all the Intuit servers went down. TurboTax® users and users of other Intuit products were unable to e-file their tax returns.[13]

"Thousands [of] last-minute tax filers were affected by Intuit's server problems on Tuesday evening, and they or their accountants may have been unable to electronically file returns. Intuit confirmed Wednesday that those problems had been resolved, and it was successfully accepting e-file returns on Wednesday. The company said affected taxpayers and tax professionals include those using ***TurboTax****,* ***ProSeries****, and* ***Lacerte****…"*

IRS News Release– IR-2007-91

Be prepared for anything. In fact, the best remedy for software crashes or bugs is to never leave anything for the last minute. Many EAs simply refuse to process returns the last few days of tax season. I also know quite a few tax professionals who refuse to e-file on the last day. Instead, they require clients to pick up their tax returns and mail them via certified mail. This ensures that the tax return will not be assessed a late filing penalty.

Set firm guidelines for clients from the beginning. You will avoid potential problems later with clients who attempt to drop off their tax returns at the *last minute.* A hard deadline, set in writing, seems to work best. For example, you can state that "any client who does not turn in paperwork by the 1st of April is automatically extended."

Office Supplies

In addition to purchasing office equipment, you will also need to order supplies. It's important that you have a good stock of basic office supplies. Most supplies are inexpensive, but you may want to spend a little more in order to secure volume discounts. You can get discounts simply by watching store advertisements and signing up for special offers. Don't buy supplies only when you run out. Whenever you see a hot deal on paper or toner, grab it! This saves money in the long run.

If you order a lot of supplies, consider opening a business account with an office supply superstore. This can give you commercial discounts on the products you order most. Also, many office supply stores will deliver your supplies for free if you reach a certain order minimum, such as $50. This saves you a trip to the office supply store when you are busiest, and it saves your back because you don't have to carry heavy boxes of copy paper.

Here is a basic list of supplies that preparers use most often. It's a good idea to create a spreadsheet and take an inventory before and during tax season. Make sure you have everything you need.

- A case of copy paper
- Ink cartridges or toner cartridge. Always have *at least* one back-up toner or ink cartridge
- Staples, tape, paper clips
- "Sign Here" flags for client signatures
- Different sizes of envelopes
- Mailing labels, postage labels
- Pocket folders or envelopes for client copies
- Postage stamps for single letters
- Calendar or appointment book
- Accordion files, manila folders, and hanging folders
- "Client Copy" rubber stamps: Make sure you always stamp the client copy of the tax return. This prevents taxpayers from accidentally mailing their copies of the tax return to the IRS (Yes, there are clients who actually do this!)

Check your supply levels often. The last thing you want to do during the busy season is to make a special run to the office supply store because you ran out of staples.

You can save money by giving clients their copy of the return on CD. You can purchase CDs in bulk for less than 10 cents apiece. This saves money, because you don't have to purchase a client folder, use toner, or paper. It's better for the environment, and it's cheaper for you in the long run.

Another huge plus—did you know that you can set a password on PDF files? Yes, it's true; you can set a password on each client's tax return that is burned to a disk. That makes PDF returns more secure than paper returns, which anyone can see if they just open the client's folder.

Setting Password Security on a PDF

You can limit access to a PDF by setting passwords and by restricting certain features, such as printing and editing. You can also restrict the **viewing** of a PDF file by setting a password in Adobe Acrobat. For tax returns, you should set a password that restricts others from viewing the file. If you own a full copy of Adobe Acrobat, you can set passwords on your PDF files. Some tax software will allow you to do this as well.[14] Two types of passwords are available:

- **Document open password:** With a document open password (also known as a user password), users ***must type*** in the password you specify to open the PDF.
- **Permissions password:** When you set only a permissions password (also known as a master password), recipients don't need a password to open the document. However, they must type the permissions password to set or change the restricted features. This setting is not as useful for security purposes, but it prevents clients from tinkering with your prepared tax return file in order to falsify records, such as increasing their AGI in order to qualify for a home loan.

You can choose to use both password settings on PDF tax returns. When you choose a password, make it an easy one to remember, such as the last four digits of the client's Social Security number.

The best part of PDFs is that it's cheaper for you, and safer for the client to use a PDF file for the client copy. Clients will be impressed with your technological savvy, and appreciate your concern about their security. It's a win-win situation for both of you.

Professionalism in Office Decor

Whether you are working from home, or have a traditional office, you cannot ignore office decor. Some Enrolled Agents minimize the importance of their office interior. This is a mistake. Customer choices are largely driven by perception. If your office is full of clutter, or filled with outdated furniture, clients will notice.

Appearance is very important in this business. It also affects what clients feel they should be billed. Establishing a professional atmosphere is imperative. That doesn't mean you need to spend a lot of money. A can of paint costs less than $20, and you can purchase a nice framed piece of artwork at a discount store for about $40. You can buy good-looking used leather couches and chairs very inexpensively.

Since you are a tax professional, your office should convey a feeling of order, detail, and contemporary elegance. Look at your office space. Does it convey order and sophistication?

If you're not sure where to start, go to a local CPA firm or consulting firm. See how they have designed their offices. Take a look at the carpeting, the window treatments, and the wall decorations. You will notice that professional firms use neutral colors on their walls. This is intentional.

Interior designers know that the colors blue, green, and gray make you feel more calm and restful. Bright colors like red and orange are known to increase heart rate and tension, which is why they are avoided in business settings.

Incidentally, though, it has been shown that red and orange are effective colors for advertising. Books with red covers tend to sell better if they are side-by-side with books that have gray, brown, or plain covers. The same goes for brochures and other ads. So you may want to use red for your brochures, but light brown for your office walls.

Use natural light whenever possible. Natural daylight increases productivity and is the least tiring of all light sources. Of course, during tax season, you'll probably be working into the night. In this case make sure that you have plenty of light. Your eyes need more light as you get older.

Incandescent lights are more expensive to use, and generally have a shorter life. But they are gentler on the eyes than fluorescent lighting. Fluorescent lights are cheap, energy efficient, and do not produce much heat. Fluorescent lighting has been linked to eye strain and fatigue. For this reason, I choose to use only incandescent lighting in my work area, but I use fluorescent lighting in the common areas.

Avoid using artificial flowers or other cheap-looking decorations. Live potted plants are inexpensive and look good. A nice mirror can make spaces appear larger. Use a nice rug to spice up drab flooring.

If you have the budget for it, consider hiring an interior decorator. Be honest about your budget, but realize that the more professional and upscale your office looks, the less clients will be inclined to quibble about their bill.

Stay Professional, Folks!

"Professionals often will display items in their office without regard to the impressions they give [clients]... Research suggests that the display of family photographs by medical doctors and by CEOs of organizations is acceptable. However, family photographs are not recommended in other types of offices. Perhaps the basis for this research finding is the common belief that one's personal life should be kept separate from one's business life."

-OfficePro Magazine

Decide Your Entry Plan

A good rule of thumb is to keep your start-up expenses under $10,000 your first year. If you are working from home, try to keep your start-up expenses under $5,000.

Develop an entry plan. It can take up to three years for you to turn a profit, so you need to figure out a way to cover your costs of living in the meantime. This is the reason why so many Enrolled Agents start out working part-time from home.

Here are some options:

1. The part-time job option.

You can work a part-time job in bookkeeping, accounting, or even an unrelated business. When your client base gets large enough to support you financially, you can drop the part-time job.

2. Keep your present full-time job.
This means that you keep your full-time job and work on taxes or bookkeeping only when you have spare time. Maybe your present job offers health benefits and you can't afford to lose them. Or perhaps you genuinely enjoy your full-time job, and only wish to do taxes as a sideline business. Whatever your reasons, if you decide to keep your full-time job, make sure you have at least ten hours a week to dedicate to your tax business; otherwise, your growth will be stunted.

3. Use loans or savings as start-up capital.
This choice seems like the riskiest, but it is also the option that will allow you to grow the fastest. Your savings should be enough to support you for at least six months. If you decide on this option, you must also plan to aggressively market yourself to the public. All of your free time should be dedicated to finding new clients. The ideal situation would be where you obtain multiple small business clients. This will allow you to do bookkeeping, taxes, and payroll, guaranteeing a steady income every month.

4. Make your former employer your *customer.*
You can also use a combination start-up method, where you convert yourself into an independent contractor for your existing employer. Later in the book, you will hear from one EA who did just this.

This method ensures that you have a built-in client base, and some guaranteed income from the very beginning. The benefit of this method is that, as an independent contractor, you are free to seek out additional clients. No matter which method you use, marketing will be essential to your success.

Larry Loses Out!

Larry Doyle completed years of accounting training and finally passed the EA exam in 2005. But he made the same mistake that so many start-ups make. He opened his practice, paid for a few newspaper ads, and waited for clients to find him. Four months later, he had exhausted his finances, and had fewer than twenty clients—not enough to support his practice or his lifestyle.

Don't repeat Larry's mistake. Watch your pennies, and don't neglect your marketing. We will discuss more about practice-building later.

Your start-up costs will vary by the amount of software and hardware you must purchase. These are only theoretical costs for a start-up tax preparation business. If you already own a computer, desk, or chair, your costs will be lower.

The following diagram does not take into account whether or not you have a home office or traditional office location. Your overhead will be higher if you have a traditional office.

If you are a student (even part-time) you may be able to get discounts on software as well. At the time of this writing, students can purchase *QuickBooks Pro* at a 50 percent discount online and at most student bookstores on campus. You can also purchase a full version of *Microsoft Office* at a 50 percent discount if you have a student discount.

I was able to purchase QuickBooks and Adobe Acrobat at a huge discount last year because I was enrolled in a college financial planning program. Even if you are taking a single college class (like web design, accounting, or even pottery!), you still qualify for hefty student discounts.

Start-Up Costs (sample)

Equipment and Software	Used or Low-End	New or High-End
Desk and chair	$75	$550
Computer	$250	$1,500
Printer	$22	$350
Software Suites	$550	$2,900
Accounting Software	$190	$1,500
Business Cards & Stationery	$75	$450
Professional Dues	$100	$250
Estimated Start-up Costs	**$1,262**	**$7,500**

A great online store to purchase student copies of software is ***www.AcademicSuperstore.com***. The software is the same, but there is a substantial student discount if you can prove enrollment in a college course. Usually you can just fax a copy of your class schedule in order to satisfy the student requirement.

Recordkeeping Requirements

The easiest way to keep all your income and expenses in order is to open a separate bank account for your business income and expenses. Shop around—there are many banks that offer free checking accounts. Choose a free account or an account with a low monthly fee. Credit unions will often offer free accounts. And credit unions have the benefit of being non-profit, so their fees are generally lower.

All of your revenues should go into your business account. All of your business expenses should come out of your business account and/or a dedicated credit card. Many part-time tax preparers choose not to open a dedicated bank account. They feel like they can continue to use their personal account, or PayPal, and that this will be sufficient for IRS requirements. This is a mistake.

Even if you work only as a part-time tax preparer, a separate bank account gives you more protection in the event of an IRS audit. A separate account shows that you are serious about your business.

For example, if you are operating your business through your personal checking account and aren't keeping excellent records, the IRS may determine that many of your expenses are "personal" rather than business expenses. The examination division of the IRS is not known for its generosity.

But wait—you really **DID** take Mary Jones out to dinner to discuss her S Corporation! All of your purchases are legitimate! You're not a tax cheat! But the IRS auditor still disallows your deduction. Now you have to go to appeals in order to fight your case, and you are going to waste more precious billable hours to defend a perfectly legitimate purchase. *Darn* it!

Do you *really* want to fight each meal and entertainment expense? Why set yourself up for argument with the IRS?
Although you may be able to successfully defend your purchases as legitimate business expenses in Tax Court, do you really want to go that far? Make your bookkeeping tasks easier from the very beginning. Get a separate bank account. If you don't have enough money to fund it at the beginning, at least get a dedicated credit card.

The dedicated credit card should be used only for business purchases. Don't use it for personal items. Use this separate credit card only for business expenses, such as office supplies, business travel, continuing education, seminars, and other deductible expenses.

Keeping track of your business expenses isn't hard when you have a dedicated bank account and a dedicated credit card. It takes the guesswork out of bookkeeping and makes it much easier at tax time. You have to keep track of all of your expenses in order to write them off on your tax returns. This is just common sense.

Even financial professionals are guilty of poor record-keeping. Don't let sloppy records keep you from performing at your best.

Every tax season, we hear about dozens of CPAs or Enrolled Agents that have been suspended from practice for *failure to file* their own personal tax returns. The Office of Professional Responsibility actually posts their names and hometowns right on the IRS website! You know what their typical excuse is? "I just couldn't get my bookkeeping done in time!"

You can go see the list of suspended practitioners at ***www.IRS.gov.*** A new list is published every year. Every year, the list seems to grow longer and longer.

Keep all your receipts. Either scan them into your computer's hard drive or keep them organized in a filing cabinet. Even the IRS admits that during an audit, most business deductions are disallowed because of poor recordkeeping, not because of taxpayer fraud.

I reconcile my bank statements once a month using QuickBooks bookkeeping software. QuickBooks is easy to use and is designed for the general public, not just accountants. It takes me a few hours every month to reconcile my bank statements. It takes very little time, and I always know what my profit and loss is from month to month.

Some old-time accountants use an Excel spreadsheet or an old-fashioned paper journal to keep track of their expenses. I learned how to keep a paper double-entry bookkeeping system in college—it's not ideal, but it works for some people. Whatever method you use, be consistent.

A good rule of thumb is to keep all records for at least three years after the date you file your tax return. If the records pertain to asset purchases (such as a computer or machinery), you should keep the records for as long as you retain the asset. Employment tax records (payroll and employee records, if you have employees) must be kept for a minimum of four years.

Business records include things like copies of invoices, cancelled checks, and engagement letters. You should also keep receipts for all of the merchandise and purchases you've made over the year. You should keep the receipts for things like shipping supplies, postage, and asset purchases. However, this doesn't mean you have to keep paper receipts.

Going Paperless

Physical records are no longer required. The IRS allows you to retain scanned copies on your computer rather than paper receipts, if you wish to go completely paperless.[15] We've already talked about the benefits of burning client copies of tax returns to CDs.

This is especially good news for people who have a lot of "heat transfer" receipts (the type you typically get at the gas pump), because these eventually fade and become illegible. My advice is to make photocopies or scans of all heat transfer receipts since they eventually become impossible to read and therefore may be disallowed during an IRS audit. It is also a good idea to photocopy carbon receipts because these eventually fade, too.

The IRS allows taxpayers to reproduce records by either electronically imaging documents [scanning] to electronic storage media, or transferring computerized books and records to an electronic storage media that allows them to be viewed or reproduced without using the original program. An inexperienced IRS auditor may quibble, but you can direct them to *IRS Revenue Ruling 97-22*, which explains how taxpayers may keep entirely paperless records. Usually, a scanned copy of the original is sufficient.

In case of an IRS audit, don't ever give the IRS original records (neither yours nor your *clients'*!). In an audit case years ago, the IRS took possession of the taxpayer's original accounts receivable records. The IRS subsequently lost the records and the taxpayer had no way to reconstruct his accounts receivable so that he could bill customers. The loss of records proved to be a financial disaster for the taxpayer. The court in the case found the IRS *was not* responsible for the loss.[16] Yes, that's right. The IRS isn't responsible for documents lost in its possession. So always make a copy, and *never* give originals to the auditor.

Choosing a Business Entity Type

Now we are going to go over some basic business information. You have to decide on your business entity type in order to set up a tax preparation company. According to the NATP, a whopping **51 percent** of all tax preparation businesses are operated simply as sole proprietorships. At the beginning, most tax preparers just file their tax returns as a sole proprietorship. That's what I did my first two years.

About 31 percent of preparers operate as corporations. The remainder operate as either a partnership or LLC. [17]

You can choose to incorporate eventually, or right away. There is no definite timeline for when you should incorporate, but the riskier your client base, the sooner you should incorporate. If you are concerned about any liability, you should either purchase liability insurance (enough to cover all your assets), or else consider incorporation (or both!). If you plan on doing a lot of representation, for example, incorporation is a very good idea.

A sole proprietorship might be fine at the beginning when you are just starting out, but once your revenues increase, so do your liabilities. Another drawback: sole proprietorships are targeted for IRS audit 400 percent more than corporations (a sole proprietor with $100,000 in revenues will be audited at a rate of 3.9 percent, while a corporation with the same revenues will be audited at a rate of about 0.70 percent—a huge difference!) For anyone who has suffered through the horror of an IRS audit, this may be reason enough to incorporate.

Now we are going to briefly review different business entity types. Some of this information will seem basic to many tax preparers, but we'll be brief. You can skip over this section if it is too remedial for you.

Sole Proprietorship

A business controlled by one person is a sole proprietorship. A sole proprietorship is the simplest business type, and the easiest to begin and set up. Income and expenses from the sole proprietorship are reported on **IRS Form 1040, Schedule C**. Profits earned on a sole proprietorship are considered the income of the owner (that's you!) and are taxed as such.

The majority of individual tax practitioners report their income on a Schedule C. This may be because so many preparers work only part-time. They may have other full-time jobs and do not plan to expand.

A sole proprietor must accept all the risks and the liabilities of the business. If a sole proprietor does not have employees, he or she generally does not have to obtain an EIN (employer identification number). You can obtain an EIN for free online on the IRS website if you don't want to use your Social Security number to identify your business (recommended).

Partnerships

A partnership is simply a business involving two or more owners. A partnership is *NOT* a corporation. Each partner contributes money, property, or labor, and shares in the profits and losses of the business. A general partner's actions legally bind the entire business. General partners are legally responsible for a partnership's debts and liabilities.

The Porter Partnership

Sammy and Jane Porter are brother and sister. Together they own the Superior Finance Company. Sammy does most of the tax returns and client interviews. Jane takes care of the day-to-day running of the office, including paying the bills and doing bookkeeping and payroll. Sammy and Jane are in a partnership. They are required to file a partnership tax return on IRS **Form 1065**.

A partnership must file an annual information return to report the income, deductions, gains, losses, etc., from its operations. Each partner includes his or her share of the partnership's income or loss on his or her tax return. Partners are *not* employees and are generally not issued W-2 forms. Partnerships are audited by the IRS at a lower rate than sole proprietorships.

So, if you are already working with a partner or a spouse, you may want to report your income as a partnership in order to lower your audit risk. Husband and wife partnerships have the option (in some cases, such as community property states) to simply report their income and expenses on the **Schedule C**. Although this may be easier, it is a poor choice to report business income this way. Partnerships should always report income and losses on **Form 1065**, even if they are husband and wife partners.

"LLC" - Limited Liability Company

A Limited Liability Company (LLC) is a relatively new business structure allowed by state statute. LLCs are popular because, similar to a corporation, owners have limited liability. An LLC is when one or more individuals form an entity with the liability protection of a corporation, but the tax benefits of a partnership.

Some financial advisers are in love with the LLC. As a rule, attorneys seem to prefer the LLC while tax professionals (such as CPAs and EAs) seem to recommend corporations. There are drawbacks and benefits to both entities. An LLC is a legal entity. Therefore, if you wish to form an LLC, seek competent legal advice.

Corporations

Unlike partnerships and sole proprietorships, corporations are considered entities separate from their owners. A corporation is treated just like a person, with its own identifying number and its own tax return. If you form a corporation, the corporation will "pay" you as if you are a regular employee. One of the biggest drawbacks to a corporation is the yearly tax return requirement—even if you don't have any revenues! You must file corporate tax returns EVERY SINGLE YEAR, even if you don't have any income.

If you form a corporation, you will have to pay the fees to incorporate and file yearly corporate returns whether or not you make a dime. If you fail to file corporate returns, the IRS will fine the corporation for each failure to file.

The benefits of incorporation have to do mainly with liability protection. Incorporation also helps owners manage their cash, and it shows a modicum of professionalism that a sole proprietorship does not. All the larger accounting firms operate as corporations or LLCs. But you do not need to incorporate in order to prepare tax returns.

Corporate tax law in the United States is very complex, and beyond the scope of this book. Sit down and talk to someone about it before you incorporate. Get advice from colleagues. In some states, corporations are required to pay franchise fees in order to simply exist.

Chapter 3

Marketing and Advertising Dollars

"Really high spending on advertising is an admission of failure."

—Ward Hanson,
Author of: *Principles of Internet Marketing*

Marketing for Tax Professionals

Many accounting professionals find marketing distasteful. You might find it immodest. You might hate drawing attention to yourself. Accountants are generally a quiet bunch, so you might not enjoy public attention. This is a feeling you must overcome if you are going to succeed. Marketing is part of every successful business plan.

Tax preparation is a customer-oriented business. You will be working with the public every day. Even if you are the best Enrolled Agent in the world, clients are not going to beat a path to your door if they don't know how to find you.

EAs agree that the best clients are usually referrals. Building your tax business through referrals is great, but what happens when you have no clients to begin with? When you first open your practice, you have to develop it through marketing and advertising. Once your tax practice is established, you will start to develop referrals and you'll be less dependent on advertising and marketing.

One important note: Even though the United States Supreme Court passed a landmark decision in 1977 allowing professionals to advertise their services, tax professionals are still required to follow the advertising guidelines in IRS Circular 230. This means that you cannot make any misleading claims. You also cannot make any legal claims, (unless you are an attorney).

Your advertising should focus on your own strengths, skills, and knowledge. Emphasize any specialties or training you may have. Do not disparage competitors. Emphasize quality rather than price. It is best not to mention price at all, although you can make statements like, "We offer a free initial consultation."

Remember, you are trying to target the best client, not a person who is trying to price-shop.

The key to your marketing plan is to understand your own strengths and weaknesses. The best way to do this is to clearly describe yourself, your services, and your qualifications in writing.

Create a short bio; you will need to do so for use on your website anyway. Describe all of the services that you offer. You can create a "services menu" and include it in all your brochures.

If you prefer to bill on a flat fee basis, you may want to outline basic fees or an hourly rate for tax preparation and bookkeeping. If you charge per form, you can advertise based on that.

Think of a slogan that describes your practice. Your slogan should be short, memorable, and grammatically correct! Slogans are good marketing centerpieces for advertising campaigns. You can put your slogan on all your business cards and promotional material. Here are some examples:

"*Better Business Ventures, Inc.* is a financial engineering firm for individuals and small business owners"

–Better Business Ventures, Inc.

"*Delfau Tax & Financial Services* believes in the flat-fee tax return. Here you'll find no surprise hourly or add-on fees when it comes to having your tax return prepared!"

–Delfau Tax & Financial Services

What Clients Look for in a Tax Pro

This next section is designed to teach you how to understand your potential customer. Right around tax time, dozens of financial magazines will come out with articles on how to find a good tax professional. Year after year, the ideas are the same. Taxpayers are all basically looking for the same qualities (unless they're dishonest, and you don't want those clients anyway). There are five basic principles that you must follow if you are going to succeed in marketing your practice.

1. Understand Your Audience.

Who is your target customer? What type of client are you trying to attract? Do you prefer small businesses and corporations? Or do you do a lot of RALs? Do you want to work with seniors, Hispanic taxpayers, or domestic partners? All of these markets need different marketing approaches. Understand the type of client you want from the very beginning and go after it. Then, if you happen to attract other clients through referrals (which you eventually will), you can decide to expand later.

2. Use Straight Talk Instead of IRS Jargon.

Your clients are not stupid people, but they appreciate when you explain things in simple terms. Don't just say something like, "This is how Congress decided to do it this year," or something equally dismissive.

Clients like to understand why they are paying a certain amount of taxes; this is especially true when they owe at tax time. If you notice that the client is getting a nice deduction, explain it to them. They will appreciate your feedback and guidance. Everyone likes to save on their taxes. Understanding tax deductions that can save them money is one thing that clients actually enjoy.

3. Give Year-Round Tax Advice.
Explain to clients that you are available year-round to answer their questions. You are not always selling a service—sometimes you are selling peace of mind. Respond to calls within twenty-four hours even during your busy season. Even if you don't have an answer for them yet, let them know you are working on their issue. This shows clients that you care.

4. Explain Your Fees Carefully and Concisely.
Don't "nickel and dime" your clients. Charging for copies, postage, and other small items just infuriates people. Instead, include these small charges in your overall bill, rather than itemizing every $2 to $3 charge. Offer estimates, or consider a flat fee for certain services. Marketing research has shown that one of the major issues clients have with their tax professionals is the breakdown about their fees. Clients don't necessarily want something cheaper, but they want to understand what they are paying for. Consider creating a spreadsheet or another invoice that clearly explains the services you provide.

5. Explain the Benefits of Your EA License.
Studies have shown that taxpayers are absolutely terrified of the IRS. In some cases, taxpayers have admitted they're more afraid of the IRS than death itself.[18] Be sure that your client understands that you can represent them in the case of an IRS audit. Tell clients that you have accountant-client privilege in non-criminal tax matters. This helps ease fears.

Cheap Marketing Tips for EAs

The best source of clients is **referrals**. If you provide excellent service year after year, your client base will grow. But how do you get those clients through the door so you can start that wonderful word-of-mouth advertising? At the beginning, it may seem that you are just spinning your wheels trying to get new clients in the door. But don't be discouraged. There are many ways to obtain new clients without spending a fortune on advertising. In fact, some of the best techniques to get new clients are absolutely free.

1. Use (Free) Internet Classifieds

You can use Internet classifieds to find new clients, if you are diligent and check posting boards every day. A good goal is one to two new clients each month. It's easier to find bookkeeping clients this way, but you can find tax clients, too. The key is to search for businesses that are looking for part-time bookkeeping help. Even if these businesses are looking to hire an employee, send them an introduction letter and a list of your tax, bookkeeping, and payroll services. They might decide that it's cheaper and easier to use your firm for everything! That's the goal.

Start by searching job classified websites like Craigslist *(www.craigslist.com)* and CareerBuilder *(www.careerbuilder.com).* Check the "help wanted" section for businesses that are hiring bookkeepers. Contact them and ask if they would consider using a contractor for bookkeeping services. They may just decide to use you *instead of* hiring an employee!

In addition to checking the job postings, advertise your bookkeeping and tax services in online classifieds like Craigslist (*www.craigslist.org*). Posting your services on Craigslist is free in the "services" section, and usually generates at least a few leads every month. Once a potential bookkeeping client has a chance to meet you, make a point to tell them that you offer tax preparation, too.

Maybe they won't take you up on the offer right away, but I've had many instances where a bookkeeping client has turned into a great tax client.

A sample letter of introduction and list of services is included in this book. We do not recommend sending a price list. It's best to discuss your fees with your potential client when you know the scope of the work involved.

If you send out an introduction letter to twenty to thirty businesses per month, experience has shown that you will receive an average of three inquiries and at least one new client. If you send your letter of introduction via e-mail, it doesn't cost you anything except a few minutes of your time.

For maximum results, you should follow up your correspondence with a telephone call, if this contact information is provided in the ad.

2. Get to Know Other Local Businesses

Make yourself visible in the community. Attend community events (charity balls, cook-outs, fundraisers). Join the local *Chamber of Commerce* and attend as many functions as you can. If you belong to a church, synagogue, or mosque, volunteer your services and attend gatherings.

This is a great way to meet other business owners and make networking connections. Business connections are especially beneficial. Make sure you have business cards and brochures when you attend events.

Pass around your business card. Talk to people. Be smart—dress nicely and *don't drink* alcohol. Make sure your mind is sharp so you can show off your expert knowledge to anyone who asks. Collect business cards from others. Don't be afraid to send a brochure or an introduction letter to businesses that you would like as your clients—the worst anyone can say is no.

3. Get a Website ASAP!

Don't just buy a domain name and post your address and company name (I can't believe how many times I've seen tax professionals do this). These days, a nice website is a necessity. A website is a commercial that works for you twenty-four hours a day, seven days a week.

Your website should be a reflection of yourself, but it should not be about YOU. It should clearly describe the services you provide, as well as your credentials. Your website will work best for you if it is simple. It should look just like a company brochure. Focus on your qualifications, background, and clients. You may want to add a "client testimonials" page. People like to read those.

Your contact information should be easy to find. Include an address and a telephone number. People like to see a physical address, even if your mailing address is a PO Box. People want to know that they can get in touch with you easily. Are you a member of the National Association of Enrolled Agents? Good. Include links to more specific information such as your professional designations and memberships. That little tidbit of information instantly boosts your profile. That's it! Keep it simple.

I recommend that you purchase a domain and a website right away. Creating a website is easy. If you use a pre-designed template, you can do it yourself in just a few hours. If you can use Excel or Microsoft Word, you can figure out how to do your own website. Many hosting companies have simple website software that works online, and even use "drag-and-drop" editing. So stop making excuses. Get (or design) your website right away. Here are some other pointers:

Submit your website to search engines–This takes a little time, but is worth it in the long run. While you're searching for local directories on the web, you might as well submit your website to the search engines. Eventually your URL (website address) will be added to their listings anyway, but that can take many months before it happens. You'll speed up the process a bit if you submit your URL directly.

Exchange testimonials and links–Do you work with another businessperson that you like? Why not approach him or her and offer to exchange testimonials on your websites? Ask that your full name and company name be listed, along with a link to your website. That's a true win-win situation since your service provider gets the testimonial and you get a free link to your website. Every little link helps.

4. Start a Company E-Newsletter

An e-mail newsletter is one of the most effective yet inexpensive marketing tools available. As long as you have a valid e-mail address for your clients, you can send them a newsletter. A newsletter is a great way to keep in touch with your existing clients. You can purchase an easy template online and make your newsletter look professional.

An e-mail newsletter is an excellent marketing tool and serves an educational function as well. A newsletter sent electronically costs you nothing, and it gives you the opportunity to highlight your knowledge and skills to your clients. Of course, if you have an existing list of clients, send the newsletter to them, and ask if they would forward it to any friends or family who might be interested in your services.

A monthly newsletter takes a few hours of work, but the rewards can be enormous. If done correctly, it can build your reputation and prestige, and the resulting word-of-mouth referrals will more than make up for your time spent.

IMPORTANT: You should use an e-mail service to manage your e-mail marketing. There are laws against sending unsolicited e-mail of a marketing nature. Do not send your newsletters from your personal e-mail account, such as through Outlook.

Not only will you have difficulties when your list grows to more than about fifty addresses, you will also run into problems with your e-mail provider. Unsolicited marketing e-mails are known as SPAM and are against the law!

You may subscribe to a newsletter and e-mail management service such as **Aweber** (*www.aweber.com*). These services are inexpensive (starting at about $19 per month) and will help you manage your mailing list. Anyone who subscribes to your list will use what is called an *opt-in* system. This means that they have given you permission to send them e-mail about your practice.

These e-mail marketing services will also help you to make sure that your newsletter has an attractive look. The content of your newsletter should be geared toward your target audience and include information that is helpful to the readers; otherwise, they will unsubscribe from your newsletter.

How Much Should I Spend on Marketing?

Many EAs want to know how much time and money they should spend on marketing. Most consultants agree that the first year, you should expect to spend at least one-third of your time on marketing, with the remainder on actual billable hours. Even after the first year, you can still expect to spend 15 to 20 percent of your time (but not necessarily your budget!) marketing your budding tax business. Advertising and marketing is more important to a new practitioner. But many established Enrolled Agents continue their marketing efforts year after year.

If you don't have a client in the office, that's not a reason to go home or play around on the Internet. Your free time is not really "free." Your time is precious. You only have a certain number of hours in a day. Not all of your hours are going to be billable ones, so you must preserve your remaining time for marketing purposes. This ensures that you are always working to make your practice grow.

If you have free time, use that for marketing on the web. Place classified ads for your business on free posting boards like Craigslist (*www.craigslist.com*). It costs you nothing and it's time well spent.

E-mail local businesses and ask if they need bookkeeping services or tax preparation. Let them know you are available for their financial needs. Marketing includes making cold calls, setting up advertising, working on your website, networking, *Chamber of Commerce* events, etc.

After you become established, your marketing efforts may die down, but you still keep getting new clients. This is due to client referrals. Without question, every experienced Enrolled Agent I interviewed said that the best source of new clients is referrals. That's not helpful advice for EAs who are just starting out. But be hopeful! If you run your business well, one day, you will have client referrals, too.

You may get referrals right away. If that happens—good for you! Once you start generating referrals, you will find that your practice grows naturally. You should anticipate a lag time of about three to five years before your client base gets large enough to sustain continuous referrals *without* additional marketing efforts.

Targeted Direct Marketing

Direct marketing is highly effective if done correctly. You can expand your tax practice exponentially if you devote yourself to several direct marketing efforts. The most efficient direct marketing forces you to make cold calls, walk-ins, and other face-to-face contact with potential clients. Some Enrolled Agents don't have the stomach for this. Try to get over any apprehension that you may have. It gets easier with practice.

You will meet many business owners. At the beginning, keep every business card! Create a database, spreadsheet, or use an old-fashioned Rolodex to manage your client prospects. A database is important to your success! Not every business is going to need an accountant right away. Eventually, though, every business needs tax preparation and bookkeeping. Your goal is to be their first choice when they finally decide to take that step.

Let people know that you are a tax professional. Always carry business cards. If you are female, carry brochures and business cards in your purse. Every time you go to the salon, leave a business card. Do you see a bulletin board? Pin up one of your business cards.

Cold Calls and **Walk-Ins** are the most effective direct marketing techniques. This is where you actually go to a business and introduce yourself. Cold calls are those made to business prospects with whom you've had little or no prior contact. Cold calling is extremely effective in obtaining new clients. However, it is also very time consuming and you must be ready for some rude rejections.

When you first open your practice, you may want to devote a few hours every day to cold calls or walk-ins. This method has been shown to be highly effective, but some EAs find this type of marketing unpleasant. You can also combine your cold calls with direct mail; this combination-type advertising works very well. Develop a script for cold calls. It makes it easier when you are calling a business. A nice script will keep you from blabbering and it will help reduce your nervousness.

It's easier to make a cold call if you have a script in front of you. You will have much better luck talking to a manager or owner if you introduce yourself as an acquaintance or a friend of someone the owner knows.

This is why it is so important to make business connections! That way, you can say something like, "I'm Paul Smith, and I'm calling to speak with a manager about tax preparation and bookkeeping services—I was referred by Nat Jones, your architect!"

Here's an example of a good template for a cold call:

A Sample Cold Call to a Client Lead

Prospect: Good morning, Daniel's Athletic Club. How may I help you?

You: Hello. This is Paul Smith; may I please speak to the office manager?

Prospect: Speaking.

You: Good morning! I met the owner of your company, Daniel Fredricks, at the *SPCA* fundraiser last month.

I'm calling to introduce myself. I am currently doing freelance bookkeeping and tax preparation for companies like yours. My expertise is in small business payroll, QuickBooks, and tax preparation. Are there times when your current staff is overloaded and you could use a little extra help to meet payroll deadlines or need someone who really knows QuickBooks?

Prospect: Well, we don't need a bookkeeper right now, but our regular bookkeeper is going on leave next month…

You: That's fine. If it would be okay with you, I'd like to come by your office at a convenient time this week to drop off a brochure and contact information, so you'll have it if you ever need to contact me. Would that be okay?

Prospect: Yes, that would be fine. We are always looking for people we can count on in a pinch, but I'm very busy today. When you come by, just leave the information with our receptionist.

You: Great. I'll come by at 1 p.m. tomorrow.

Prospect: That would be perfect. What was your name again?

You: Paul Smith. And who am I speaking to?

Prospect: This is Mary Fredricks.

You: Thank you very much for taking the time to talk with me, Mary. Hopefully I'll be able to say a

	quick hello to you tomorrow at 1:00 when I drop off the information. Just to confirm your address, it's 123 Main Street in Sacramento. Is that correct?
Prospect:	Yes, we're on the second floor, Suite 201.
You:	Okay, great! Thanks again.
Prospect:	Thank you. (End of call.)

Contacting Former Employers

Direct marketing to former employers can be highly lucrative. Because former employers already have knowledge of how you work, they may be more inclined to hire you for bookkeeping or tax preparation. They may also prefer to hire you as a consultant because they can save money on hiring a full-time bookkeeper.

Try contacting your former employers. You may be pleasantly surprised. Even if your former employer doesn't need a tax preparer right now, he might call you in a few months. This is especially true if you offer payroll and bookkeeping.

If your former employer is an accountant, offer to do contract work. Many CPAs and EAs love using contract labor during tax season. It's cheaper for them, and it takes some of the pressure off during their busiest time. You get valuable experience and a higher hourly rate than if you were an employee. This is a great place for newly licensed EAs to start. In fact, it is how I started! You'll hear from other Enrolled Agents who got their start this way as well.

Becoming an independent contractor for another EA or CPA allows you to generate revenue even if you don't have clients. In the meantime, you can continue to search for your own clients and build your base. Believe me, there are always enough clients to go around.

Easy "Soft-Sell" Tactics

Here are some small ways you can start to get traffic on its way to your office and website. No single method will bring you a stampede of clients. But using these techniques on a consistent basis will pay off in the long run.

Soft-Sell Tip #1: Promote with Every E-Mail. Always add a signature block to all your outgoing e-mails. The signature should include your telephone number, your website, and a descriptive blurb about your practice. An example might look like this:

Sincerely, Davey Smith EA
Tax Consulting for Small Businesses
1-800-222-0000
www.SmithTaxUSA.com

Be sure to include an **active link** to your website. Some professionals even attach an e-business card—which is like a miniature version of your business card in your e-mail. Whenever you send an e-mail, it becomes an indirect advertisement for your website. Some people just can't resist clicking on e-mail links!

Soft-Sell Tip #2: Use an Online Signature. Using the same principle as an e-mail signature, include with your name a link to your website in any and all posts you may make to online blogs or message forums. You never know who might be reading your comments and just might have a burning need for your services.

Soft-Sell Tip #3: Offer Free Advice on Your Website. Encourage website visitors to "ask the expert" and submit a question to you via e-mail. Then, if appropriate, answer the question online and post it on your website. Make the question anonymous or ask permission to post the answer. This drives web traffic and allows potential clients to ask their questions via e-mail, which some skittish taxpayers prefer.

Keep Track of Your Marketing Efforts

Whatever marketing route you decide to take, make sure that you track the results. Ask every single new client how he or she heard about you. You might be surprised by the results.

One Enrolled Agent spent over $2,000 on a Yellow Pages ad only to find out that the majority of his referrals were coming from a small church newsletter with his picture on it. The advertising in the church newsletter had cost him only $89.

Another EA who spent thousands of dollars on newspaper advertising found out that most of her referrals were coming from Google AdWords, which cost her less than $50 a month. We will discuss more about Google AdWords later.

Some clients are attracted to a very narrow part of an advertising campaign. For example, perhaps you have special training in financial planning. You can highlight these special skills as part of your advertising campaign. Try to identify a niche market that you would like to serve.

Seniors, college students, real estate agents, actors, and clergy are all examples of "niche" markets.

15 Simple Practice-Marketing Tips

1. Get free media publicity. Contact your local newspaper. Let them know you are a tax expert. Send them your business card and a short bio.

During tax season, offer to submit short articles for free as long as your company information is included in the article (also called a byline). You can also contact other local media outlets and let them know you are available for interviews. Television newscasts and radio shows are always looking for good tax experts.

If you have a lot of clients asking you the same question over and over, you can bet other people in the community have the same problem. Write a short blurb about it, and send it to all your local papers. You might just hit it big and get a free advertisement for your business.

2. Practice your "elevator" commercial. You should have a short description of what you do committed to memory. This is also called the "elevator speech." It should be about one minute long—be ready to use it whenever anyone asks you what you do.

3. Buy inexpensive promotional items. Give out inexpensive nylon folders or durable key chains pre-printed with your practice information on them. You can buy nice logo-printed pens for almost the same price as non-customized ones.

4. Let them know everything you offer! Make sure every client knows all the services you provide. They might not need a bookkeeper, but maybe they know someone who does.

5. Remember clients' birthdays. There is inexpensive software that can help you do this. A nice birthday card with your signature shows personal attention to detail.

6. Make big-shot connections. If you see an important local businessperson in the news, send him or her a congratulations card. Include your business card and company information, of course.

7. Teach your knowledge. Apply to teach a course at your local community center or learning center. Hand out your business card to everyone who attends. If you have a Master's degree, consider applying at the local community college. Teaching a tax class is rewarding work that keeps your mind sharp and raises your community profile. Who *wouldn't* be impressed by a real-life college professor doing their personal return?

8. Give two. Always hand out two business cards—one to keep and another to give away. In every invoice or mailing, add a business card to the envelope. It's a cheap way to market your practice without additional cost.

9. Speak locally. Speak to local community groups, senior centers, and your local PTA (they are a non-profit right?). Offer to take questions from the audience. People love getting free tax advice. Make sure you have a stack of business cards to hand out at the end of your seminar. Smile. Make connections. People will remember you.

10. Market to current and former clients. This may be one of the most effective marketing tools in your arsenal. Keep a database of all of your current and former clients. Having a good e-mail address is like gold, because e-mail is free. In November or December, contact clients that might be good candidates for year-end tax planning. Send an e-mail and offer them a year-end consultation for a flat fee.

11. Contact your community's "Centers of influence." These are community leaders, such as your local pastor, who have influence over others. Let these influential people know that you are an EA and whether you offer financial services.

12. Send thank you cards. When you receive referrals, make sure that you immediately acknowledge the referral with a thank you card or a phone call. Even if you don't want to spend the money on postage, you can still send an e-mail.

13. Develop a media strategy. Create your own media machine. In the off-season when you are less busy, work on a press release, your biography, and get to know your local media. Let the local broadcast news stations, newspapers, and columnists know who you are. Let them know you are a specialist in "X-type of tax matters" and that you are available for interviews. Why spend thousands of dollars on print advertising when you can get the same bang for your buck simply by doing an interview?

14. In tough times, expand your practice—don't contract. The worst thing that you can do during an economic downturn is slow down. Remember that other tax professionals might be throwing in the towel. This means even more opportunities for you. Whenever you don't have clients, use that valuable down time to find new ones. Reach out to find bigger and better clients.

15. Use free online video marketing to boost your visibility. It's true. *Free publicity* is the best advertising. And anyone can create a video these days—just use an inexpensive camcorder or even a cell-phone camera! Even if you have NO video editing skills, I've seen production fees for custom video "trailers" for as little as $150. Create a little video about your tax practice, what you offer in financial services, and tell the audience a little bit about yourself.

Post the video on YouTube, your website, and e-mail the link to your entire client base and everyone you know. It's an easy way to boost your visibility. Tax pros aren't known for their marketing savvy! So get over your shyness and differentiate yourself from all the other tax pros in your area.

People are much more likely to seek you out if they can see what you look like and see your warm smile and comforting voice. Money issues and tax problems scare people. Why not take the time to create a little video that shows the personalized service you have to offer?

Public Relations

Public relations is a different type of marketing. Perhaps you are already heavily involved in your community. Sometimes your activities will be related to your tax business, and sometimes they won't. But the main idea here is to get involved and establish networking connections with other businesses and individuals. Sometimes this type of silent marketing is the best publicity.

One of the best examples of this type of "silent" marketing is when tax professionals get involved with non-profit organizations. Volunteer for local charities. Get involved with sports clubs or church groups. If possible, try to become a board member. This allows you to be in a position where you can inject valuable financial guidance to the group. This is especially true for non-profits; as many of us know, they are often desperate for financial advice.

You may believe that you don't have to time to devote to these organizations, but the opposite is actually true. You may be very busy during tax season, but everyone has at least a few hours a week to devote to a good cause. And if you are spending $5,000 a year on advertising, why not save that money, work a little less, and let your volunteering become an indirect marketing tool?

People love to talk about work. This is especially true for small business owners. Never miss an opportunity to mention that you do financial consulting and tax preparation. Community networking is some of the best advertising you can do for your business, and best of all, it's free.

Networking with Organizations

Because making business contacts through networking is so important to new businesses, it's important that you set aside some money to join at least one professional organization. If you have not already done so, I recommend that you join the *National Association of Enrolled Agents*, which is the largest national organization for EAs. The NAEA is over 11,000 members strong, and they have chapters in every state. In some states, like California, there are multiple chapters.

When you join, you'll receive marketing tips and valuable business advice. It's an excellent resource for EAs. You'll get information on events, continuing education, and networking opportunities. Being an NATP or NAEA member also entitles you to great discounts. For example, NAEA membership entitles you to a discount on popular reference books like the *QuickFinder* or *The TaxBook*.

Membership also entitles you to discounts on "Errors and Omissions" insurance from various companies. These discounts may cover the cost of your membership. There are other memberships that add credibility to your business; the organization is essentially lending its credibility to you as a member.

Daniela's Story

Daniela was a single mother and an Enrolled Agent working for a small CPA firm. She decided to start a tax practice on the side in order to earn some extra money. But she didn't have any money to advertise or promote her business. She also worked out of a home office, and she didn't want strangers in her home.

Daniela volunteered at a local animal rescue organization. She mentioned that she was an Enrolled Agent with experience filing non-profit tax returns. Within six months, she was the treasurer of the organization, and she had filed two years of delinquent returns for the organization (at no charge). She did all the bookkeeping for the animal shelter on QuickBooks. All of the board members were impressed by her comprehensive financial reports. When Daniela attended meetings, she was always nicely dressed and professional. When board members asked her for financial advice, Daniela was warm, friendly, and had a business card ready.

She volunteered for the organization for six years. In that time, she had over sixty-five referrals from staff members and board members. These referrals are all people that Daniela knows and trusts, so she is not afraid to have them in her home. Her tax practice continues to grow organically from referrals. Although she continues to work full-time at the CPA firm, she now earns an additional $23,000 a year from her part-time tax preparation business. And all of her clients came entirely from public relations, not from traditional advertising. You can also build your own practice this way.

Chapter 4

Client Selection: Basic Advice

"As a general rule, the client who pays the *least* will expect the *most*."

-Inside CRM,
Top Ten Ways to Fire the Client *From Hell*

Be Choosy with Clients from the Start

From the start, choose *quality* over *quantity*. A single high-income client who consistently pays on time is worth twenty sporadic late-paying clients. Keep your job easy from the very beginning, and listen to your instincts.

Every now and then, you are going to come across clients who are just awful. Maybe they pay late (or not at all) and maybe they are demanding, unreasonable about those demands, or just flat-out rude.

Enrolled Agents need to have honesty and integrity in order to be successful. You should also look for clients that share these qualities. A client that asks you to do something questionable will have no qualms about not paying his or her bill!

From the very beginning, be choosy. Trust your gut feelings about a client—they are usually right. If you feel that a client will not pay his or her bill, you are probably right. Either decline the engagement, or request a retainer up-front. This is especially true in the case of delinquent taxpayers. No matter how much they quibble, do not release their tax returns unless they pay you first.

When a client comes to you with five years of unfiled tax returns, make sure you have a standard engagement letter ready. Let them know that there will be a retainer up-front, and that you will start work as soon as they pay the retainer. If they complain, be firm and let them know this is your company policy. Remember that some of these people are experts at getting services for free without paying for them. If the client doesn't come back with the retainer or his records, you know you probably wouldn't have gotten paid anyway.

Although I have accepted delinquent filers before, I always let them know that payment is expected when they pick up their tax returns. If the clients complain that they don't have the money, I return their originals and offer to extend their tax return so that they can file later when they can afford it.

I admit I have fallen for "sob stories" in the past, and agreed to file the tax return by the deadline even though I hadn't gotten paid. Usually these clients would promise to pay "as soon as they got their refund." In almost every case, with seriously delinquent taxpayers, I was unable to collect my fee. The client mysteriously disappeared.

Remember:
An IRS tax-cheat will eventually cheat *you*, too.

Deadbeats jump from one tax preparer to another, using the same sob story every year.

Resist accepting clients who are low-level or have the possibility of being slow-payers. Set high standards for yourself and your client base, and you will rarely need to suffer through the hassle of collections. Aim high from the start and you won't be scrambling to get paid over the long term.

Give personal attention to your best clients—they are the ones who are going to generate the best referrals. Successful people tend to travel in the same circles. Provide personalized and frequent contact with the best clients. They will refer other good clients to you, too.

The best way to avoid payment problems is to avoid problem customers. Slow-pay clients are the neediest! Learn to recognize warning signs of a bad client at the very beginning:

1. How long have they been in business? Most businesses fail in the early years, so the longer a firm is in business, the better the chances of receiving timely payments.
2. Do they want to haggle over price? If a client complains that your rates are too high, they either don't value what you do or are strapped for cash. Usually it's the latter.
3. Does the prospective client want you to do work with an unreasonable deadline? Are they always in a hurry, pressuring you to complete a task at the last minute? They likely do not handle their other payment obligations on time either.

How to Fire a Client

Sometimes, you have a client that is just more trouble than he's worth. Don't be afraid to "fire" clients who are repeatedly slow about paying their bills. Remember, your time is valuable, too. Every minute spent doing collections is wasted time that could be spent on marketing or billable hours.

Try to weed out clients who are slow-paying or end up in IRS collections every single year. Sometimes you can make a client go away simply by raising your fees. A former CPA that I worked for used to jokingly call this his "jackass fee." It works.

Either the bad client goes away, or they pay a higher premium for your services, which is fair since they are taking up more of your time anyway. Here are some good ways to "fire" those problem clients:

Problem: The Procrastinator
Solution: Set a Firm Deadline

The procrastinator is the client who asks you to do his return "ASAP," but comes to you with incomplete (or non-existent) records. Then, when you ask for the information, it takes him until April 15th to get it. The procrastinator only responds to an ultimatum. Give this client a firm deadline for the information. Do it in writing. Send an e-mail and write a letter. If he fails to comply, refuse any more work and refer him elsewhere.

Problem: The Penny-Pincher
Solution: Double Your Fees

This is the tried and true method for firing those penny-pinching, needy clients. You know the type: they say that they are "broke," and you see that they made $200,000 last year. They argue about the bill, call you ten times a day, and refuse to pay when they pick up.

These clients respond best to dramatic fee hikes. Double their fees for all the extra trouble they cause. Keep doubling their fees every year until they leave. It usually only takes one fee hike.

Problem: The Fibber
Solution: Refuse the Engagement

The fibber is a clean-cut, upstanding, church-going client who doesn't believe he should pay taxes. He's a "silent" tax protestor; which means he cheats on every tax return, but doesn't brag about it. He drove up in a new BMW, but his income from self-employment is only $7,500? His records are a complete fabrication, and you *know* it. Smile, and hand him back his paperwork. No amount of money is worth this risk.

Problem: The Loud and Discontented
Solution: Stop Contact, but Gently!

This client is never happy. You might have saved him $10,000 in taxes, and even discounted your bill, and he still finds something to complain about. These clients are tricky, because they typically have big mouths. They love to complain—about everything!

But be careful…you don't want this crankster to badmouth you all over town! Don't call, don't e-mail, and don't send a tax organizer. Raise fees. If all that doesn't work, and he still returns to you for tax preparation, you can play the "attorney referral card":

"I'm very sorry, but your tax issues are so complex, and you have so many questions, that I would feel more comfortable recommending you to a tax attorney."

Problem: The Needy One
Solution: Invoice for Every Call

The needy one is the client whose paperwork is perfect, always pays on time, and then calls you every day for advice on every business decision he makes.

The needy one wants all his financial decisions to be perfect—which means he can't even buy a pack of gum before calling you to consult about it. The needy one thinks that the $250 fee they paid for tax preparation entitles them to free, daily phone consultations.

The only way to fight this type of client is to be straight. Tell him, "This call is free, but if you need any additional consulting, it will be billed at our regular hourly rate." If he calls again, send him a bill for a "phone consultation." The phone calls will stop.

My True-Life Deadbeat Client Story

My husband's friend, Felipe[19], was being garnished by the IRS. Felipe owed thousands of dollars in delinquent taxes. I reviewed his tax returns, which had been prepared by a tax franchise (I won't say which one). I found numerous errors, missed deductions, etc. I prepared five years of amended tax returns. These discovered errors transformed his sizable tax *debt* into a very small refund. In the end, I figured I saved Felipe about $6,000.

He had some money trouble, but Felipe was friends with my husband, so I didn't worry about it. In the end, I did $1,700 worth of work and filed the amended returns on good faith. After filing the amended returns, I sent Felipe the bill. Months went by without payment. I asked my husband if Felipe had received my invoice. Felipe admitted he had, and he was just waiting for his refund check to come in.

A year later, I still hadn't seen a dime. Rather than make my husband uncomfortable, I stopped badgering him about the delinquent bill, and I decided to write off the invoice. It was a great learning experience for me. Never again will I prepare tax returns for a delinquent filer without payment up-front, even if it's a close friend or a family member—unless I don't intend to get paid.

Amazingly enough, the following year, Felipe sent me his tax documents by mail. I was astounded. I promptly mailed his documents back and told him that I don't work for free. I suggested that he find another preparer. That was the last I heard of him. Needless to say, my husband and I do not socialize with him anymore.

Client Retention

Of course, the majority of your clients will be wonderful clients that you want to *keep!* Client retention is at the core of practice management. Clients will not recommend you unless they are happy with your service. Don't assume that once you have a client, he or she is going to stay enamored of you forever. Your marketing efforts should always include some component of client retention. It is always easier to retain a current customer than it is to go out and find a new one.

An established client is more likely to recommend you to family and friends. They also take up less of your time. It is easier and faster to do a tax return for an established client than a new client. You don't have to do an extensive interview every year; you just need to find out what has changed. This translates into a higher billable rate per hour for you.

Even during your busy time, make sure that you deliver personalized service. Always be pleasant and friendly, and don't act like you are "rushed," even if you are! Your customers will pick up on your attitude.

Chapter 5

S-Corp Conversions: the Ethical Money Maker

"The income tax has made liars out of more Americans than golf."

-Will Rogers

Expand Your Revenue Stream

Everyone knows that a corporation is a great entity structure for clients who want to take their businesses to the next level. For many small businesses, incorporation is the best way to manage cash flow, reduce audit risk, and increase liability protection.

The biggest benefit with S Corporations (over C Corporations) is the pass-through treatment that S Corporations receive. In this respect, they are taxed more like partnerships, but they give clients additional legal protections that a partnership does not.

S Corporations are audited at a much lower rate than sole proprietorships. For some clients, this is reason enough for them to convert over! Currently, the IRS audit rate for sole proprietorships (Schedule C) is about 4 percent. The IRS audit rate for S Corporations is about 0.7 percent—less than one percent! This is a good thing!

In addition, if your client's corporation is audited, the audit will be handled by IRS field auditors. A field audit ensures that the audit will take place at your office, not at an IRS building. Field auditors have more experience and frequently have formal accounting backgrounds. This makes intelligent discussions easier.

Have you ever had to deal with an IRS auditor straight out of IRS "boot camp"? It isn't pretty. Every EA has a funny story about trying to explain basic tax law to a novice IRS employee. A field audit ensures that you won't have an IRS newbie fumbling through your paperwork and asking one idiotic question after another.

In the following interview, you will hear from Owen Arnoff, a successful EA in Northern California. Owen's practice has a 100 percent positive review rating on CitySearch (*www.citysearch.com*), an online opinions website where people can post their opinions about their neighborhood businesses. At the time of this printing, Owen's practice had an incredible nineteen positive (5-star) reviews, and not one negative review! Amazing in itself, but a testament to how good client service becomes public knowledge these days.

This is a good lesson for those who might want to kick a client to the curb. Watch how you treat your clients—even the worst ones! Anyone can go online and post a nasty review that can be impossible to remove.

Owen started as a licensed insurance agent and moved into the field of taxation naturally. Now his practice offers a wide range of services to the public, including tax, bookkeeping, and insurance products. Owen is a big proponent of the S Corporation conversion, and he recommends it often. This boosts his bottom line because he then prepares multiple returns for the client (personal, payroll, and corporate). The clients are better served because they save on self-employment tax and have added liability protection.

It doesn't take much convincing to get clients to agree to an S Corp conversion, especially when they know that their risk of IRS audit goes down, while their liability protection goes up! The tax savings usually covers the cost of the conversion and the additional tax returns.

It's a win-win situation for everybody!

Interview with Owen Arnoff, EA ATP

Better Business Ventures, Inc.

www.BetterBusinessVentures.com

Professional Designations: Enrolled Agent, Accredited Tax Preparer, CTEC Registered Tax Preparer, Certified QuickBooks ProAdvisor, Life & Disability Insurance Agent License (California, Texas, Maine), Real Estate Agent License (California), Series 7 General Securities Registered Representative

Your online reviews are just incredible! How do you get such glowing reviews?

Owen: Well, I have a very loyal following. We work very hard to help our clients out and be very proactive. We look for ways to save people money on their taxes. The tax code is really complicated for the average person. Most people are not armed with competent financial advice.

What do you feel is the best way to get clients?

Owen: For me, the best client is a referral. The client has heard from someone else, "Hey, this tax pro saved me thousands of dollars because he knew about this tax credit." I have a loyal group of clients; some of them have become friends of mine over the years.

How did you start in the tax business? How did your practice develop?

Owen: Well, in 1996, I was hired as the CFO for a local franchise. It was a mobile paint repair company. And they were very successful—it was a multi-million dollar franchise. I got to know all the employees because I was overseeing all the accounts receivable. All the bills would go through a central office and then I would pay all the franchisees out of that. The owner of the company was business-savvy, and he could recommend tax-saving strategies as well.

We encouraged the franchisees to incorporate and pay themselves a regular payroll. The business kept growing, and when I left, the business was doing millions in sales. But the position was stressful, so I went out on my own and started my financial business. And the franchisees used my services. I did their payroll and bookkeeping. One thing led to another.

So you became a tax preparer at that point?

Owen: Yes, I researched the programs available, signed up for a course, and became a CA Registered Tax Preparer (registration is required in California).

How many years have you been in private practice?

Owen: I've been in private practice for six years.

You're a big fan of the "S Corporation." Why don't you tell us a little bit about that?

Owen: When someone comes in and is a "Schedule C" filer, I usually convert them over to an S Corporation if they have $20,000 or more in taxable income. It's better for the client, and it's better for me. I then do their corporate return, their personal return, and I'll usually do their payroll, too. And I'm licensed as an insurance agent so I'll often do a group health plan for them, too. I also have a securities license so I can do retirement planning.

Not every client converts over, but I try to offer everyone the choice.

That might be why your audit rate is so low. The audit rate for corporations is much lower than for sole proprietors.

Owen: Yes, I've only had four IRS audits in all my years of practice. The audits were for current clients of mine—but the tax returns were for prior years and not returns that I had prepared.

The IRS is going after taxpayers that file the Schedule C. I went to a seminar in Baltimore, and the former head of the IRS Appeals department was speaking. He said that the majority of the "tax gap" is due to the Schedule C. The IRS is on to them. They are going after Schedule C filers pretty aggressively.

When people convert over, it automatically creates a payroll client for me, too. I charge about $1,000 a year for monthly payroll. I have one employee that does all the S Corp conversions. He's my right-hand man.

Do you use traditional advertising?

Owen: I've done some. I've done a whole bunch of different things. I've tried radio advertising, and I've tried print ads. That didn't work.

I'm a "Certified" QuickBooks ProAdvisor, not just a ProAdvisor. I have to pass a test each year to prove I'm "competent" in each edition. Sure, they collect the same $695 per year, but being certified is just a small step above.

I got listed on the Intuit ProAdvisor website. That generates a lot of calls. One of the clients that contacted me through the ProAdvisor site said to me one day, "You know, you really ought to do taxes professionally." I wasn't sure at that point if I really wanted to do it.

I use a lot of Google AdWords (online advertising). I'll be honest with you, though. The BEST advertising I've ever done—the one that's paid off the most for me in terms of "leads" is a website called Bookkeeping Help.com (*www.bookkeepinghelp.com*).

It's owned by a couple down in Georgia who has somehow been able to maintain a website that is number one in Google's natural search listings for any type of bookkeeping word search. So when users search for "bookkeeping help" on the Internet, that site is always at the top of the list.

So let's say someone searches for "Sacramento bookkeeper" on Google. When they go to Bookkeeping Help.com, I am the first one on the list because I was the first one in Sacramento to advertise with them. So I've gotten sixty or seventy clients from that one source.

I built my practice though word-of-mouth and through Internet advertising. I also purchased dozens of domain names, which all point to my main website.

I also purchase other tax practices. Last year, I bought a small tax practice. It was an older tax preparer who was ready to retire. Through a broker, I found the practice. It was 150 clients, and I retained about 100 of them. The problem was that most of the clients were in a city about fifteen minutes away and I am in Sacramento.

Which software suite do you use?

Owen: I use Intuit's ProSeries. I have used Lacerte in the past, but it was (and still is) waaay too expensive for my needs. Even ProSeries is expensive, but you get what you pay for. What I like and need is a suite of products (rather than a single product) because I don't just prepare individual returns.

From what I hear, quite a few practitioners use Drake Software, which I tried out, but found very difficult to use.

I noticed that you have a very interactive website with video.

Owen: I contracted with a company called *I Speak Video* to do a video for me. The video pops up and makes the website more attention-grabbing. I also have a counter that allows me to know when someone is visiting my site. I also can see what search tool they used to find my website. Last week, it was really funny—someone was on my site, and when I checked, they had typed "Best tax preparer in Sacramento." That's how they found me.

It wasn't five minutes later that I got a phone call. She's coming in tomorrow.

That's incredible!

Owen: I get a lot of referrals from my website. I don't get a lot of hits—maybe only thirty per day, but for a tax practice, thirty hits a day is a lot!

When did you decide to become an Enrolled Agent?

Owen: I feel that if you really want to be a professional in this business, you really need to be an Enrolled Agent.

I wholeheartedly agree, so when did you decide to become an EA?

Owen: About four years ago, I decided to take the Enrolled Agent exam. I purchased books and studied all summer. I like live courses, though, so I went down to San Francisco and took a three-part live course. I passed all three parts the first time.

Do you belong to any professional organizations?

Owen: Yes, I belong to all of the major tax organizations: NATP, NAEA, NSA, CSEA—I belong to all of them. I get e-mails from all of them. I read them; I try to keep up- to-date on what is happening in the field. I also subscribe to the Kiplinger Tax Newsletter and I read that pretty religiously. This helps me keep my clients informed. I just started a blog over the weekend. I'm going to try and keep posting information to the blog.

So what is your office like?

Owen: I have employees. Up until July, I had six people working for me. I had a couple working for me, and they moved to Portland, Oregon after the season was over. My wife works for me. She's trained to do taxes, but she mainly does data entry and bookkeeping. I have another tax preparer that does a lot of payroll.

Everyone works as a team. But nobody in this office signs a return except for me. I review all the tax returns before they go out.

Do you have anything else to add?

Owen: Here's the biggest tip that I can give a new preparer, and one that I have learned only with experience.

DON'T WORK FOR FREE. Get a retainer up-front.

My learning curve is *over* in this respect. I'm a professional, and I want my clients to pay me for my services. I use engagement letters for every single representation case I do. If you are going to do a representation case, get a retainer, especially if you can see the client has money problems. It makes sense—if they're deadbeats to the IRS, they're going to be deadbeats to you.

Chapter 6

Protect Yourself from Claims

"The best measure of a man's honesty isn't his income tax return. It's the zero adjust on his bathroom scale."

-Arthur C. Clarke

Everyone Makes Mistakes

Everyone makes mistakes. We're all human. You have to protect yourself from claims, follow practices that will limit your liability, and carry liability insurance. This won't eliminate the risk, but it will help mitigate serious issues.

Most tax professionals carry some type of liability insurance. Typical insurance coverage is designed to cover claims that are a result of practitioner errors or negligence.[20] The most common claims are for mistakes that occur during the preparation of tax returns.

On average, claims settle for $15,000 to $40,000. Few claims exceed $500,000, but it does happen.[21]

In most cases, policy coverage is between $100,000 and $2 million. All CPA firms and attorneys carry liability insurance as a matter of course. Practitioners who sell insurance products or mutual funds typically purchase a separate policy to cover those activities. Insurance, real estate transactions, and securities transactions typically require an additional policy.[22]

In order to qualify for Errors and Omissions insurance, the majority of your income must be from tax preparation, bookkeeping, or other accounting services.

Protect Your Practice!

All Enrolled Agents are concerned about the possibility of making mistakes. Mistakes cost money—in legal fees, IRS penalties, or interest. You can help reduce your legal risk by following some very basic guidelines. Learn how to protect yourself from the very beginning and you will have an easier time when (and if) you finally do make a mistake! Here are some excellent practice management tips from Dineen Huft, an Agent/Broker at Placer Insurance Agency:

Smart Practice-Management Tips

1. *Always* use engagement letters.

No exceptions. And be careful when providing services for family members. Use the same practices as you would for a non-family client.[23] Did you know that *family* claims against EAs are some of the most common types of claims?

2. Stick to what you know.

Stay within the area of your expertise. If you are uncomfortable in a certain area of tax law, either refer the client out, or consult a professional who specializes in that area of taxation. It's impossible to be an expert at *everything.*

3. Write it down.

Maintain a phone log, even when the conversation is between the receptionist and the client. How many Enrolled Agents have had a client "forget" to pick up their tax returns on time, only to blow the filing deadline?

4. Confirm details in a letter.

Put things in writing. After speaking with your client, follow up or confirm the conversation in writing or e-mail. This creates better communication. And make sure you keep a written record of the conversation in the client's file.

5. Organize your files.

Organize your client files consistently. Having each file handled consistently will allow you to find and avoid mistakes easier. Reconsider taking on clients who are disorganized.

6. Tell business clients to bond their employees.
Encourage business clients who have bookkeepers to purchase an "Employee Dishonesty Bond." This bond protects the client from theft /embezzlement by their employees.

Understand Your Insurance Policy

Professional liability policies should be reviewed each year.
Do you have adequate coverage? Consider the following when choosing:

- The personal assets of you and your spouse (if married)
- The wealth and complexity of your clients' situations—do you work on a lot of corporate tax returns, or high income taxpayers? Consider your risk based on your clients' assets, too.
- Are you covered for prior mistakes? Will work you have done in the past be covered? There is most always a significant time delay between when the alleged mistake was made and when the mistake is *discovered.* Make sure your policy has coverage for *prior acts.*

If you retire or sell your business, will there be coverage for the work you did prior to the retirement or sale of your business? Make sure your policy covers you for past years, (also called *tail coverage*) since it is often a long time before an error gets discovered, sometimes many years.

Each policy has rules regarding when you are responsible for contacting the insurance carrier about claims. Most "Claims Made" policies will require you to notify the company if you think there may be a claim.

The Most Common Claims Against EAs

The most common claims seem like very simple mistakes, but remember that simply the failure to file an extension on time can cost your client thousands of dollars in late filing penalties alone!

I asked Placer Insurance Agency about the most common claims they had seen over the years against Enrolled Agents. The following is their response:

- **Failure to file tax returns** (Example: the EA forgets to file a payroll tax return or a personal tax return for a client). Failure to file a timely extension is also a common claim.
- **Depreciation errors**
- **Premature application of 10-year averaging**
- **Miscalculation of sales tax owed to state**
- **Juxtaposition of numbers errors** (This is simply when you transpose one number or read a form incorrectly—who *hasn't* done this at some point!)
- **Divorced couple** (Choose one, both, or none)
- **Disgruntled family member** (Watch out for this one! Nothing breaks up family harmony faster than money troubles!)
- **Countersuits** (Retaliatory claims by disgruntled clients are the most common type of claim. The Enrolled Agent sues the client for unpaid fees, and then the client turns around and sues the Enrolled Agent for "negligence" or work not completed.

Trust your instincts—a deadbeat client might end up coming back to bite you in the end. Try to avoid this type of client from the very beginning.)

Real-Life Claims Filed Against EAs

Here are some examples of real-life claims and legal actions against Enrolled Agents. I thank Dineen Huft at Placer Insurance Agency for providing these examples. All of the names in these cases have been changed.

The Wandering Decimal

Fran Jones, EA prepared a tax return for a client who had substantial pension income. The actual pension income for the taxpayer was $44,150, but Fran entered the amount on the client's tax return as $4,415. The IRS caught the error, and the taxpayer paid the additional tax.

The insurance company settled the case on behalf of the tax practitioner for $3,116, which was the amount of the penalties plus one-half of the interest.

Angry About Retirement Funds

Client Jane Smith consulted with Harry Doe, EA about a stock transaction tied to her retirement funds. Jane subsequently withdrew the funds and failed to roll them over into another retirement account. Jane was charged a hefty penalty for early distribution.

The client sued Harry Doe, EA, because she alleged that the Enrolled Agent did not properly advise her of the potential penalties with the transaction. The Errors and Omissions insurance covered the cost of the attorney and the litigation costs. Jane Smith did not receive any damages from Harry.

Capital Gain Miscalculation

Bill Trent, EA, advised his client that he made an error on his capital gains percentage. Bill had calculated 20 percent and it should have been 28 percent. The taxpayer was unaware of the error. The additional amount of taxes owed would be approximately $143,000.

Bill calculated interest and penalty of approximately $6,500. The E&O Insurance Company advised the EA to have the client pay the taxes and send in an estimated amount of interest. The insurance company advised Bill to send a letter to the IRS asking to have the penalties abated.

Thankfully, the IRS abated the penalties in this case, so the taxpayer was only liable for the actual tax and the interest. The taxpayer still had to pay $3,333 in interest. This claim was eventually settled for $2,946 by the insurance company.

Chapter 7

Income and Pricing Methods

"**Marketing** is the key to everything. Doing the work is the easy part. It's the *selling* that's the hard part. You can never sit back. Every day you have to sell yourself again."

-Sue Rugge,
Co-Founder of the *Information Professionals Institute*

How Much Should I Charge?

The most important factor in deciding how much to bill your client will be YOU. If you set a higher value to your skills, your clients will pay. Some tax preparers prefer to bill a flat fee based on services. Either way, you should always require an engagement letter and bill your clients according to the services agreed upon in that document. If your client wants to add services, make sure your client understands that additional services mean additional cost.

It is difficult to say how much income you can expect from your tax practice. Your success will depend on numerous factors, including your location, which services you offer, and the number of clients you have.

A small town will probably not have the same opportunities for growth that a large city might have. On the other hand, you may have more intimate contacts in a small town and be able to drum up steady business from clients that you already know.

Although what constitutes a "good income" is highly subjective, an Enrolled Agent can earn a higher hourly rate working independently than for an employer. This is true for full-time tax preparers as well as part-time preparers. Even if you choose to keep your current job, you can still carve out nice additional income doing bookkeeping, tax preparation, or payroll part-time on the side. In fact, this is how most EAs get started.

Salary Earned as Employees

According to the Bureau of Labor Statistics, the average *unenrolled* tax preparer makes an average hourly wage of $16.89, or about $35,000 per year. The average bookkeeper makes about $9 to $15 per hour working as an employee.

Freelance bookkeepers (independent contractors) generally charge about $30 to $60 per hour.

A licensed professional (such as a CPA or Enrolled Agent) working for an accounting firm makes an average of $62,550, or about $30 per hour. This is the amount typically earned as an employee. There is a big disparity based on location, with the lowest-paying states being Maine and Arkansas, with an average annual income of about $42,000. The highest paying states for licensed preparers are Connecticut and Alaska, at just over $70,000 per year.[24] These are the average income ranges for licensed tax professionals who are employed.

Self-Employed VS. Employed Tax Preparers

The salary numbers for self-employed preparers are much different. The average tax practice generates about $135,000 in gross receipts per year. This average takes into account all tax practices, both part-time and multi-office practices.

Sole practitioners (without employees) average $60,000 in billings per year (this number includes full-time and part-time preparers). Year-round tax practices generate more revenue than part-time practices. Enrolled Agents who offer multiple financial services, such as payroll and bookkeeping, tend to make more money overall. Income also varies according to the number of tax preparers[25] employed by the practice and how many years the practice has been in business.

Charging for Representation

Representation work is billed out differently than tax consulting. Some tax professionals prefer to charge a flat fee for representing a client before the IRS. Others charge an hourly rate against a retainer.

Every EA that I interviewed requires a deposit *up-front* for representation. The average retainer for representation is a few thousand dollars. The retainer amount varies by the complexity of the case. A simple **Form 1040** audit where the taxpayer has excellent records might only be $1,000. A horrific trust-fund penalty case might be in the tens of thousands of dollars. You have to estimate the amount of time you think the case will take and bill accordingly.

You may want to bill on a monthly basis. Tax professionals will often agree to a monthly payment plan for representation work, after the initial retainer has been agreed upon. At the minimum, you should demand at least sixty days worth of payments in advance.

So, for example, if you agree to a $300 monthly payment for ongoing audit work, then make sure you get at least $600 up-front before starting any of the legwork for the audit. Some EAs include automatic billing in their contracts.

Offer the client an agreement to charge his credit card every month. This ensures that you get paid and a client doesn't need to worry about sending you a check. As many of us know, many of these cases take years to resolve and the last thing you want is to wait years before you get paid!

Don't be the Cheapest

You may think that you will get more business by keeping your hourly rates low. And you may well be swamped with low-paying work if you insist on being the cheapest in town, especially if you do high quality work. But you won't be making any money and you'll be exhausted for your efforts.

If that is what you want, there are plenty of volunteer organizations that are in desperate need of your help! If you don't care about making a profit, then volunteer work will be far more satisfying than running your own business.

Don't ever try to be "the cheapest in town." Call around; ask local CPA and EA offices what they charge by the hour. Make up a scenario. Tell them you are self-employed with a Schedule C, or say you have an S-Corporation. Most of them will give you a ballpark range. Find out how much they charge for bookkeeping, too. Use these numbers as your guide, and plant yourself firmly in the middle. Don't ever try to be the "cheapest."

Most new preparers (and even some experienced ones) are afraid to charge a reasonable rate for their services. One of the most common pitfalls for new Enrolled Agents is undervaluing their own worth. Charge a fair amount for what you provide from the very beginning.

Don't be tempted to accept every client, either. The clients who haggle over price are often the most difficult to deal with, or are the worst for paying late. Don't ever haggle over price. Your office is not a flea market. Value what you do, and your clients will, too.

One thing that I think CPA firms do well is that they are unapologetic about their hourly rates. Tax attorneys don't apologize for their fees, either. In fact, most attorneys take courses on how to get over the guilt of billing their clients large sums of money. There's nothing *unethical* about turning a profit!

We're in business. That's all there is to it.

If you present yourself professionally to your clients and have the experience and credentials behind you, it is appropriate to charge accordingly. If, on the other hand, you have limited tax experience and training, you may want to consider subcontracting work from other bookkeeping services or CPA firms before seeking your own small business clients. Either way, you have valuable services to offer those who hire you.

If you present yourself professionally and also have a professional office environment, people will pay a premium for your services.

Don't shoot for the gutter. Always shoot for the sky.

A side note: Don't ever "put down" another tax professional. Don't make personal attacks. I've seen some practitioners degrade other preparers and this is always a mistake. Comments like, "Oh, Joe Smith drinks too much and that's why he can't prepare a decent tax return," or even worse, "Paul Jones has pancreatic cancer and he can't possibly prepare your tax returns. You better start looking for another preparer right now." This is a definite no-no. It is acceptable, however, to comment on the *quality* of another professional's *work product,* especially if you see errors.

Point out the mistakes. Give your opinion of the tax return (not the preparer), and then let the client reach his own conclusions. Usually they will say what you were thinking all along, but were too polite to point out! This makes *you* a tax pro and it prevents you from looking petty.

CPA firms and attorneys charge a premium for their services, and so should you. The Enrolled Agent license is one of the most prestigious in the world. Remember that, and don't shortchange yourself.

Jenny's Story

Jenny started out working for a CPA firm right after she passed the EA exam. The job gave her valuable experience, and it also taught her that her degree of professionalism would influence how much she could charge for services.

While Jenny was working for the CPA firm, people would call and price shop. Some balked at the hourly rate, which was over $300. But the head of the tax department, a CPA, once told her, "We don't haggle over price. Not ever. This isn't a flea market. Clients that argue about their bill don't really want good service. They want the cheapest price in town. And that's not really the type of client we want."

The firm had thousands of clients and eleven CPAs in the tax department alone. Jenny remembered one client in particular. It was a multi-million dollar partnership with hundreds of partners, including multiple foreign partners. The bill for that single return was over $35,000.

Wouldn't *you* love to have a client like that?

Average Preparation Rates

Your profit potential will increase according to your hourly rate and the number of clients you have. There are some national averages. According to Intuit's 2007 preparer survey, the average fee for a professionally-prepared Form 1040 was $130.

Some tax preparers choose to charge by the form. Some even charge "per page," regardless of the tax return's complexity. I don't recommend this method, but it is popular with a few EAs.

For those charging by the form the average rate for a **Form 1040** with a **Schedule A** is $165. In addition, a **Schedule C** will usually increase the price of the tax return by $65 or more. The addition of a **Schedule E** usually runs about $45 and up.[26] Corporate and partnership returns are billed at an average rate of approximately $400 to $600 each, depending on the complexity.

Self-employed EAs generally bill their services out at a rate of $100 per hour. The average billable rate for self-employed CPAs is $150 per hour. This varies greatly by location. The average hourly rate for bookkeeping varies from $30 to $60 and is mostly due to location. The average flat fee for monthly bookkeeping is $350.

If your hourly rates are significantly higher and your practice is doing well, there is no reason to lower them. This is especially true if you offer a niche tax specialty, such as clergy or foreign earned income. However, if your preparation rates are significantly *less* than the ones listed here, examine why that is. Are you trying to undercut your competition? Are you trying to be the cheapest in your city? Are you trying to compete with H&R Block? All of these are losing propositions. Don't ever try to be the cheapest, and don't try to compete with chains. As an EA, you offer a unique service. Bill accordingly.

Perhaps there are other reasons for your low rates. Perhaps your practice is in a depressed neighborhood. Perhaps your clientele is mostly low income or retirees on Social Security. If that is the case, seriously consider moving your practice location. It might seem like a huge step, but location is so important to your success. So is the appearance of your office.

Don't try to save $100 on rent and lose a $1,000 high income tax return because your potential client is turned off by your grubby strip mall office.

Also, examine your client base. Can you develop a profitable niche? How about going after some business clients? These are all practice-expansion techniques that can help increase your bottom dollar without increasing your workload. Why do ten low-profit tax returns for $50 bucks each, when you can do one high-profit tax return and make the same amount of money? Work *smarter*, not *harder*.

Here are some examples of what you can expect to make as an independent tax preparer. The assumption is that you'll have at least one or two bookkeeping clients. Here are some scenarios based on a five-day work week:

Realistic Practice Scenarios

Example A (low estimate): If you have one client per day (5 clients per week) at an average preparation fee of $100 per tax return, this equals 500 X 52 (weeks) = $26,000 per year, or $2,166 per month. If you can add just **two** bookkeeping/payroll clients at a monthly fee of $250, you can increase your yearly income by $6,000! This would increase your yearly gross income to $32,000 per year: **$26,000+$6,000=$32,000**.

Example B (average estimate): If you have two clients per day (10 clients per week) at an average preparation fee of $125 per tax return, this equals ($125 X 2 X 5) X 52 (weeks)= $65,000 per year, or $5,147 per month. If you can add **three** bookkeeping/payroll clients at a monthly fee of just $300, you can increase your yearly income by $10,800! This would increase your yearly gross income to $75,800 per year: **$65,000+$10,800=$75,800.**

Example C (high estimate): If you have three clients per day (15 clients per week) at an average preparation fee of $150 per tax return, this equals ($150 X 3 X 5) X 52 (weeks)= $117,000 per year, or $9,750 per month. If you can add **four**

bookkeeping/payroll clients at a monthly fee of just $350, you can increase your yearly income by $16,800! This would increase your yearly gross income to $133,800 per year: **$117,000+$16,800= $133,800.**

As you can see by the numbers, all of the scenarios use conservative tax preparation fees and a reasonable monthly flat rate for bookkeeping. The key to your success in this business is two-fold: build your client base, and charge a reasonable fee. If you can learn to do that, you can be on your way to a bustling tax practice in no time.

Chapter 8

How to Offset Seasonal Income

"You know, gentlemen, that I do not owe any personal income tax. But nevertheless, I send a small check, now and then, to the Internal Revenue Service out of the kindness of my heart."

-David Rockefeller

Become a Full-Service Provider

Income from tax preparation is seasonal. The majority of Enrolled Agents receive most of their income in three months out of the year, which causes "cash flow" issues for the rest of the year. Revenue from tax preparation peaks during March and April, with another bump in October and September when most extensions come due. Exceptions to this rule are practitioners who specialize in estates and non-profits, both of which are usually filed on a fiscal-year basis.

The best way to combat this seasonal spike in income is to diversify your services. Become a full-service provider. Listen to your clients, and diversify your services based on their needs.

Eighty-five percent of small businesses have fewer than twenty employees. These small businesses usually want the easiest solution to their bookkeeping and financial reporting requirements. Most small businesses would love to have one place to go for payroll, tax preparation, sales tax reporting, bookkeeping, and financial statements. The best part about offering these additional services is that they generate revenue all year round.

Tax preparation is a good way to generate large revenues and a steady client base. On the other hand, bookkeeping and other financial services provide a stable yearly income and generate year-round revenues.

Why not make your practice a "one-stop" shop? Always explain all the other valuable financial services you offer. Have a brochure ready, and make sure every potential client knows that your office is their "one-stop" shop.

Bookkeeping services are a great money-maker all year round and a great way to fatten your pocketbook in the lean months after tax season. Most EAs admit that they have at least a few "bread and butter" clients that they bill throughout the year for bookkeeping services; this helps stabilize their cash flow during the slower months.

You can even consider offering insurance services and real estate representation, if you obtain the necessary licenses to do so. You will read interviews from Enrolled Agents who offer these additional services later in this book.

Most Enrolled Agents charge their clients a flat monthly fee for bookkeeping and payroll. This can range anywhere from the low end of $50 per month to thousands of dollars a month for a large client (such as one with multiple business locations). The average monthly bookkeeping fee is $350. Of course, this will vary dramatically based on the number of hours you spend doing the books.

Expect to spend about five to ten hours a month doing the books of an average small business. Billable hours will vary based on the client's size, number of transactions, and your skills as a bookkeeper.

As your skills improve, so will your speed, and you will be able to take on more clients. You may even need to hire a professional bookkeeper to pick up the slack. Many EAs employ full-time bookkeepers. If you can hire a well-trained bookkeeper who will also answer the phone and make appointments, you kill two birds with one stone. If you find a bookkeeper who also has good customer service skills, treat this person like gold. Offer a nice salary from the very beginning, and you will save money because one exceptional employee can usually do the work of two people.

You can also do what many accounting firms do—farm out your bookkeeping to independent contractors and bill accordingly. An easy way to find good contract bookkeepers is to ask other tax professionals in your area. You can also place an ad on Craigslist or other job posting boards. Clearly state that the job is a contract job.

Remember, if you are paying contract labor rather than an employee, you cannot direct where or when the contract bookkeeper performs his or her duties. Many tax practitioners prefer to farm out repetitive bookkeeping or data entry work. You can also decide to hire part-time or temp help only during your busy season.

Before I became an Enrolled Agent, I did this type of contract bookkeeping work myself. I was able to come and go as I pleased, as long as the bookkeeping was done within a certain time frame. Sometimes I took files home, and I carried a USB drive that held my back-up files.

While some CPA offices offer small business bookkeeping, they typically charge rates higher than the average small business can afford. CPAs might charge between $100 and $350 dollars per hour, even for bookkeeping. One CPA told me once that if the client was "too lazy to do their own bookkeeping, they deserved to pay their regular hourly rate, since an hour of bookkeeping took just as long as an hour of tax preparation." He also told me that he charged a premium to clients who brought in dirty, disorganized receipts.

The remarkable part is that these clients continued to bring in those same old boxes of receipts year after year, even though they were told that they could save hundreds of dollars simply by organizing the receipts themselves. They just didn't want to do it.

As a rule, tax professionals hate dealing with "messy clients," but don't forget that these clients can be very lucrative! As long as you are straightforward about your fees and tell the client that they will be charged for bookkeeping, you shouldn't feel guilty about charging for your time.

Even a financial incentive, such as saving $300 on bookkeeping fees, will not be enough for clients to do the bookkeeping themselves. After all, they have been neglecting their books the entire year, and there is no real motivation for them to begin organizing their finances right before tax time. Disorganized clients are generally willing to pay for you to clean up their financial mess.

Don't turn down a bookkeeping client just because they use a CPA or tax attorney for their tax return preparation. Money is money. Who knows? Maybe they will consider your tax preparation services in the future.

People often confuse formal accounting with tax preparation and bookkeeping. Assurance services and non-assurance services differ greatly. Tax preparation and other financial services are not to be confused with formal accounting, which involves interpretation of official financial statements. *Assurance* services are offered by CPA firms, and typically carry a great deal of liability. Assurance services include financial statement audits and reporting mandated by the Sarbanes-Oxley Act (SOX).

Fewer than 2 percent of businesses in the United States require this type of financial reporting. The remaining 98 percent are small businesses or midsize businesses that need the type of financial guidance and services that you provide as an Enrolled Agent.

Non-assurance services include bookkeeping, tax consulting, IRS representation, and management consulting services.[27] All financial services are interrelated and cannot exist without one other, but they are not the same. Enrolled Agents keep client records and report client information to the IRS.

Many CPAs work exclusively on financial reporting and do little (if any) tax reporting, although there are CPAs who specialize exclusively in taxation. Some CPA firms do not do any individual taxes, and focus exclusively on corporate or non-profit work. There are attorneys who specialize in taxation, too.

Bookkeeping services are a great way to increase revenue and also ensure that your tax clients are doing everything that they should be doing in order to comply with current tax laws. Good bookkeeping helps you and helps the client. It's a win-win situation for everyone involved.

Become a QuickBooks ProAdvisor®

A great way to increase your referrals and credibility in the marketplace is to become a Certified QuickBooks ProAdvisor®. This is a certification offered by Intuit, the manufacturer of QuickBooks, Lacerte, and ProSeries tax software. To sign up, you will need to call 1 (888) 236-9501. You have to talk to an Intuit employee in order to sign up for the program. Unfortunately, you cannot sign up online.

We are covering the ProAdvisor program because many of the EAs that I interviewed for this book are also ProAdvisors. If you offer bookkeeping services, you must also purchase an updated version of QuickBooks every year. You might as well become a ProAdvisor and get the additional client referrals that the program provides.

The ProAdvisor courses are available online and are self-study. The primary certification course is designed for bookkeepers and accounting professionals who already have a good working knowledge of QuickBooks and bookkeeping. A college degree is not required.

To become a Certified QuickBooks ProAdvisor®, you must complete the online testing after each section and receive a score of 85 percent or better. You will have to renew your certification every year in order to stay active at the top of the ProAdvisor referral list.

Generally, certification takes about sixteen hours, but the time and investment is well worth the effort. That's because once certified, each ProAdvisor is given a free listing and customizable profile page in the QuickBooks searchable directory, which Intuit markets aggressively. That means referrals for business from clients based on your geographic location.

Some EAs report that they obtain client referrals *each month* from the Intuit ProAdvisor website. Once your bookkeeping clients find out that you do taxes, they may decide to use you for all of their financial service needs.

Once you become a ProAdvisor, you can even offer QuickBooks training and company set-up for a fee—many tax professionals offer QuickBooks consulting and they charge an average of $40 to $90 per hour for QuickBooks training.[28]

If you have a bookkeeper on your staff, QuickBooks training is something that can be relegated to him or her. The billable rate is much higher that the typical wage for a bookkeeper, so you are able to make a tidy profit and also offer a valuable service to your clients that helps them manage their finances. Not bad!

ProAdvisors are also given a priority technical support telephone number and early notification of new programs and upgrades.

Offering Payroll Services

Tax professionals usually have strong feelings about payroll. Some offer payroll services, but dislike actually doing payroll. Some professionals have dozens of payroll clients and love offering the service. Payroll is a year-round service, so you (or an employee) would have to be available to provide the service all year. That's a drawback as well as an advantage.

Offering payroll services means that you will have steady income all year round, but you will be unable to take long vacations away from the office in the off-season like many tax professionals enjoy doing (unless you have employees who can do the payroll in your absence).

Most Internet payroll companies have special discounts just for accounting professionals. This makes it easy to offer an affordable payroll service to small and mid-sized businesses. There are numerous payroll companies that offer plans to accounting professionals. Shop around and see which one offers the best option for you.

Offering Property Tax Consulting

Enrolled Agents are *income tax* professionals, but don't forget that there are *other* types of taxes out there—not just income tax! Consider expanding your practice by doing property tax consulting. Municipalities are loath to reduce a property's assessed value (even if the actual value plummets), because it reduces their tax revenues. Taxpayers are appropriately incensed when their property tax bill arrives and the "assessed value" is hundreds of thousands of dollars higher than the actual market value.

Property tax consulting can be a lucrative business. Most homeowners and business owners don't know how to appeal their property tax assessments. You can take a property tax consultant course and learn how to do property tax assessment appeals, which often result in thousands of dollars in savings for the client.

There are numerous courses and books available to help you learn how to do this. Some firms even specialize exclusively in this type of representation. If you have a client with a $500,000 home or business property, you may save him thousands of dollars simply by filing an appeal.

Many consultants charge based on a percentage of the amount of property tax *savings* to the client. This can reap thousands of dollars in income for a single successful appeal. Consider adding property tax consulting to your practice, especially to your high-end clients or clients who own commercial property.

Business Plans and Budget Forecasting

If you are an Enrolled Agent with a business background, consider offering detailed business plans and budget forecasting to your service offerings. Small business consulting can be highly profitable work. A good financial plan can help your client manage his or her money, time, and even control stress.

Here's a secret that most EAs already know: *most small business owners start their businesses without a competent business plan or a budget.*

There are warning signs that you can look for that indicate when a business needs consulting help.

If your client comes in and complains of:

- Frequent cash shortages
- Rising credit card debt to cover business expenses
- High staff turnover or low employee morale
- Difficulty meeting payroll obligations
- Late product delivery or botched jobs
- Continual inventory problems
- Difficulty managing the payroll trust fund (a BIG red flag!)
- A steady increase in costs without a corresponding increase in revenue

These are all indicators of a client who needs expert financial guidance. The best time to approach clients about these services is when you are doing their compliance work. Don't be pushy—just drop a hint.

Dropping a Subtle Hint

EA: You know, Jim, it looks like you really lose control of your spending the last half of the year. You don't even have enough to pay your income tax due. What happened?

Client: Yes, well, I had money in the bank and I decided to buy a car…and then the wife and I decided to take a vacation…I guess I did make some bad money choices last year.

EA: Well, I think you are a good candidate for budget forecasting. I can help you find out where all your money is going. I can help you take control of your spending. My professional services include budgeting and forecasting solutions. I charge $450 for a detailed financial plan. Think about it and call me when you are ready.

Just plant the seed. Nine times out of ten, your client will contact you for a consultation. This is your chance to be a rescuer, and it is one of the most rewarding services that you can provide. Clients are often amazed when they see their initial reports—they say, “I had no idea I was spending $850 per month on dining out!” You can help them get their lives back on track.

There are numerous software companies that offer budgeting and forecasting software for accounting and tax professionals. Lacerte offers forecasting software in addition to regular tax software.

The next interview is with Gabrielle Fontaine, PB. Gabrielle is a professional bookkeeper who also has a tax practice. She does tax returns, bookkeeping, and QuickBooks consulting. She also has a popular newsletter and does Internet seminars to boost revenues and publicity. Her business model is extremely successful because she uses every available resource to help grow her bookkeeping practice.

Interview with Gabrielle Fontaine, PB

www.TheFreelanceBookkeeper.com

Professional Designations: Professional Bookkeeper and Advanced Certified QuickBooks ProAdvisor®

Why consider adding bookkeeping services to a tax practice?

Gabrielle: Bookkeeping and taxes go together like peanut butter and jelly! They naturally complement each other.

Business clients are required to have adequate bookkeeping records in order to file their tax returns. This is a necessary evil as far as many small business owners are concerned, and the only reason they keep records at all!

Even those who attempt to keep good records often have little discernment about what is important to track financially and what is not, both for tax purposes and for business management and growth.

These realities, however, open opportunities for you to offer additional services surrounding bookkeeping to your existing clients. And, of course, that means additional income for your business.

Are bookkeeping services a good way to boost profits year-round?

Gabrielle: Yes, because tax services are seasonal, bookkeeping services provide you with a predictable revenue stream, since they need to be performed on a weekly or monthly basis. It is only natural to offer this much-needed assistance to your business clients. It will also make your life a lot easier when it comes time to prepare their tax return! If you choose to pass those savings along to your clients, you'll have fans for life.

What about clients who try to do their own bookkeeping? What do you say to them?

Gabrielle: In truth, many small businesses attempt to handle their own bookkeeping, with poor results. Since you already recognize the importance of tracking the money flowing through a business for tax purposes, you are in the perfect position to identify where, if your clients improved their recordkeeping procedures, they would save on taxes. This makes it easy for you to broach the topic as well as justify the cost of providing bookkeeping services to your tax clients. Many entrepreneurs will immediately recognize the value and convenience of what you propose. It's an easy sell.

One of the biggest challenges freelance bookkeepers face is building trust with new clients. You, as their tax professional, already have that rapport and trust. If the client is in need of help with his books, it will feel more like you are doing him a favor than trying to up-sell him on additional services.

How about referrals?

Gabrielle: As you begin to offer bookkeeping services, inevitably your clients will mention you to their colleagues and friends. And if you provide quality service at a reasonable rate, you will get new clients who are only seeking bookkeeping services as well. In turn, these new bookkeeping clients may become new tax clients, too.

Thus starts the synergistic cycle between both tax and bookkeeping revenue streams in your business.

Of course, you will want to thank your clients for any referrals they send your way, possibly showing your appreciation with a thank you note or even a small gift card to encourage additional referrals.

Any tax practitioner should be able to offer bookkeeping too, right?

Gabrielle: While bookkeeping records are needed to prepare tax returns, if you are trained in one, it does not mean that you are automatically proficient in the other! Having an understanding of how income and expenses are reported to tax authorities does not mean that you know how to properly book the day-to-day transactions of a business using a double-entry bookkeeping system.

Do not attempt to offer bookkeeping services unless you have an adequate understanding of full charge bookkeeping and the entire accounting cycle. Attempting to handle small business bookkeeping without adequate training would be a serious disservice to your clients that could get you into hot water.

The biggest complaint many CPAs have about freelance bookkeepers is that anyone can hang out her shingle and call herself a bookkeeper whether she has any qualifications as a bookkeeper or not. This complaint, in my experience, is justified. Many so-called bookkeepers have no experience or training in proper bookkeeping procedures, and do much more harm than good to their clients' books. Bookkeeping is not mere data entry.

What does it take to get proper training?

Gabrielle: The good news is, learning double-entry bookkeeping is much easier than keeping up with the ever-changing tax laws. The principles of bookkeeping are static and can be learned easily through self-study or online training programs, as well as at local community colleges.

There are also several online and correspondence certification courses available, with the Certified Bookkeeper designation being the most recognized (offered through the American Institute of Professional Bookkeepers– *www.aipb.org*).

Although a degree in accounting is certainly helpful, it is not necessary. What is necessary is being able to properly record the day-to-day operations and produce monthly and yearly financial statements that accurately express the standing of the businesses you serve.

What do you think of QuickBooks?

Gabrielle: If you decide to offer bookkeeping services to your clients, you will inevitably encounter the most popular bookkeeping software program for small business– QuickBooks®. It is worth your while and nearly essential to become familiar with this program.

Similar to the differences between taxes and bookkeeping, just having bookkeeping knowledge does not mean that you are proficient in using QuickBooks properly. In fact, it is not uncommon for CPAs and trained bookkeepers who have no experience with QuickBooks to struggle with the program and even foul up their clients' books in short order! That's because QuickBooks was designed to be user friendly to non-accountants, encouraging small business owners (or their employees) to do the books themselves.

The problem arises in the power of the program. While it is, in fact, user friendly, it has become more complex as it has gained popularity and functionality to handle more and more complex business recordkeeping needs. What this means to you is that you should not attempt to "wing it" if you will be providing professional bookkeeping services to your clients using QuickBooks software. You will need a solid working knowledge of the program.

I highly recommend joining the QuickBooks ProAdvisor program provided by Intuit (the makers of QuickBooks). Not only does the program include a lot of training resources, it also provides ProAdvisors who achieve certification the opportunity to market their services on the QuickBooks national database, which is a great way to build your presence on the Internet and pull in new clients. Intuit also provides practice marketing materials inside the ProAdvisor membership site. The ProAdvisor program is well worth the investment.

What about other services?

Gabrielle: There are additional revenue possibilities that open up should you choose to pursue certification in QuickBooks and provide expert consultation services to your clients. These include integrated payroll services, QuickBooks training, troubleshooting, support and maintenance to name a few. In reality, QuickBooks consulting is a whole profession in itself.

How can EAs pick up long-term bookkeeping clients?

Gabrielle: In all likelihood, your first few bookkeeping clients will come from your own business tax preparation client base. They will be easy to identify because you will already know if they are struggling with their recordkeeping efforts based on the quality of their source documentation presented for tax preparation.

Simply let them know that you are also able to assist with their bookkeeping work, whether that be reconciling their accounts each month, taking over their payroll processing, or even handling the entire recordkeeping process for them.

The trick about adding bookkeeping services to your tax practice is not attempting to take on too much all at once. You only need one or two clients to start. More clients will naturally come your way if you provide high quality service, simply due to word-of-mouth referrals.

Like tax preparation, bookkeeping can be time consuming. But it needs to be done every single month. So my best advice is to keep some variety in the types of clients you take on. Have some that need you every month, and some that need you on a quarterly basis, or an as-needed basis.

You do a fair amount of QuickBooks consulting. What would you advise practitioners to do in order to offer this service?

Gabrielle: If you pursue the QuickBooks consulting route, you can provide support and training to help your clients who are already using QuickBooks software. Help them to streamline and improve what they are already doing. There is actually a huge demand for QuickBooks training both in groups and on a one-on-one basis. Providing training services can be quite lucrative.

Another choice is to offer a quarterly data review to make sure your clients' books stay clean throughout the year. This will lead to additional clean-up services and training as well.

Add to that a quarterly tax planning review, and you will create a very attractive and comprehensive service for your clients who are interested in growing and improving their business. Of course, adding these services will help to even out your own cash flow in the process.

What do you do to get your name out into the community?

Gabrielle: Networking with colleagues, including CPAs and other EAs may open doors for pulling in additional bookkeeping and QuickBooks consulting clients. Let them know about the services you offer and look for ways to complement the services they offer. Looking for opportunities that are mutually beneficial and not competitive will produce better results and build strong strategic alliances.

Another great way is to do local seminars that will attract colleagues and small business owners alike. So, again, QuickBooks training is a natural for this tactic. You can do either free or paid workshops through your local Chamber of Commerce or Small Business Development Center.

Because there are so many small businesses that are in real need of help when it comes to recordkeeping, you should be able to attract a few clients and begin to build a significant revenue stream.

Grow your client base slowly and deliberately and you will have a lucrative, well-rounded business with a stable, more constant cash flow.

Chapter 9

Get Lucrative Representation Clients

"A man who represents himself has a fool for a client."
-Abraham Lincoln

Boost Profits with Representation

Everyone knows that IRS audits are unpleasant. Some tax practitioners avoid taking these representation cases because they are often messy. Everyone has seen those clients who come in with a giant box of receipts, zero recordkeeping, no bank statements, and multiple years of unfiled returns. What a headache!

Not every client is going to be neat and organized. We knew that going into this business, right? The "silver lining" on these untidy cases is that they can be very profitable.

Delinquent filers often come in during the off-season, after they get "hate mail" from the IRS. This makes it doubly profitable because you can dedicate your time to these delinquent returns outside of your regular tax season hours.

Instead of referring these cases out or turning these clients away completely, it is best to develop a firm strategy to deal with them. Schedule a sit-down consultation to review the client's individual situation.

Everyone is going to be different, but there are a few things that you should always do. For clients who are delinquent with the IRS, make sure you **ALWAYS:**

- Use an engagement letter.
- Get a retainer up-front (no exceptions!)
- Be truthful with what you feel you can accomplish with the IRS. Don't promise the moon and the stars.
- Always give the client a reasonable time frame for when the issue can be resolved.

The wheels of the IRS turn very slowly, so the client needs to understand that their tax case might take months or even years to resolve. Be straightforward from the beginning and you will have fewer problems later.

Taxpayers will appreciate it if you are honest with them, even if you cannot resolve their tax issue. Tell them that they can depend on you, but don't make wild promises you can't keep. And for audit cases, always get money up-front. If they don't leave a retainer, tell them not to leave their records. It's as simple as that.

Some tax practices even specialize exclusively in representation work. Audit cases are going to appear, so why not increase your client base and your profits by advertising IRS representation services?

Now, in addition to walk-ins and referrals, you can also "chase down" these lucrative cases. There are many ways to seek out these clients. You can advertise on the web using Google AdWords, a highly effective Internet marketing technique that is easy to use, even for beginners. You can target your advertising to just your immediate area or make it nationwide, and you can set daily "maximums" for your advertising dollars, such as $5 per day. I have used Google AdWords myself with great success.

You must have a website in order for the advertising to work, however. And if you don't have a website yet—GET ONE! You can't really do business without one these days, and it's the cheapest form of advertising out there. My website costs me $55 per year, and it works for me twenty-four hours a day. Where else can you get so much for so little?

Delinquent filers often won't voluntarily seek help. They will ignore IRS notices for months or even years, and only contact you when their wages finally get garnished. Or they may get suckered into bogus "tax resolution" firms that take their money and offer little help with the IRS.

These clients feel they have no one to turn to, and they don't trust anyone. They might be embarrassed or ashamed.

These clients will typically accept professional guidance if it is offered to them kindly. You just have to learn how to find them. Once you have found them, the next step is to learn how to handle these types of cases and get paid.

Problems During An Engagement

Once you accept an audit case, you are dealing with the IRS. You are the only line of defense between the IRS and the client. There are some common pitfalls to watch out for during an engagement. When you start the audit process with the IRS, always make sure you get all the details. Always come prepared to the interview. The more organized you are, the more appreciative the auditor will be.

1. Verify your IRS agent.
IRS employees are masters of confusion, and you don't want to get halfway though a field audit just to discover that you are talking to a special agent and your client is under criminal investigation!

If your client is under investigation by the Criminal Investigation Division, you have a duty to inform your client immediately.

Since EAs and CPAs do not have the right to the confidentiality privilege in criminal cases (only attorneys do), this may be a situation where you need to step back and perhaps withdraw from the engagement.

> **Can I See Some ID, Please?**
>
> Watch out that you are not dealing with a special agent of the IRS Criminal Investigation Division in a case which you believe is being handled as a routine audit or collection matter. If a special agent is investigating your client, your client has a serious problem. It is ***the goal*** of the IRS special agent to put your client in ***jail.***
>
> **-Robert M. Kane, Jr.**
> LeSourd & Patten, P.S.

2. Get an original signature.
Make sure you have a **Form 2848** with a wet signature.[29] Although the IRS must generally accept photocopies, I have had at least two IRS agents quibble about the lack of original signature on a document (never mind that the entire world is going paperless while the IRS is still drowning in paper).

3. Always use Certified Mail.
Don't use regular mail when dealing with the IRS. It only takes one instance—one failure to respond to a ninety-day notice—to kill an engagement and possibly set your office up for a lawsuit. The IRS is a messy place.

They lose documents—a lot. Make sure that you protect yourself and your clients by using Certified Mail every time you communicate time-sensitive information to the IRS.

Successful Client Triage

David Jones[30] is an Enrolled Agent who runs a busy tax practice in Southern California. About 30 percent of his practice is representation work, which includes IRS collection, IRS audits, Offer in Compromise, and other negotiations with the IRS.

David employs three trained tax preparers who also answer phones and do the simpler tax returns during the filing season. All of David's staff members are trained *by him* how to answer calls from clients who are seeking IRS representation. The preparer asks pertinent questions from a list, and writes it all down in a folder for David to review. When David gets the file, he determines if the case is one that is worth accepting (David does not accept tax protesters or tax shelter cases).

David tells a staff member to contact the client and schedule a meeting. The client is asked to come in thirty minutes early to fill out a questionnaire and also drop off his paperwork. If the client is a referral from an existing client, the initial consultation is free. If the client is new, the payment for the consultation is paid in advance of the meeting.

During the initial consultation, David discusses the realistic expectations for the engagement and gives the client an engagement letter. The engagement letter is about two pages long and outlines all the client's responsibilities during the engagement. The letter also clearly states that work will not begin until the retainer is received.

The All-Important Engagement Letter

It is amazing how many tax pros do not use any kind of written agreement in the normal course of doing business. Even many small to medium-sized CPA firms do not consistently use engagement letters with their clients. If you don't have an engagement letter, you could end up arguing with the client endlessly about what was promised and for what price. This is especially true in representation cases, which are notoriously difficult to collect upon if you don't have a retainer up-front.

My advice is to use an engagement letter with every client. It can be simple, with just a few notes and the agreed- upon price. Or it can be complex, with detailed explanations and even clauses for how a dispute will be settled should one arise. The messier the audit case, the more detailed your engagement letter should be.

The purpose of having a contract BEFORE the working relationship begins is to avoid the risk of problems and misunderstandings in the course of doing business.

Some tax professionals resist using engagement letters. You might feel it will scare away business or indicate a lack of trust with the client. If you request an engagement letter from a client you have known a long time, it may seem awkward. Perhaps you've never used any formal engagement letters in the past, and you feel that your client will be taken aback by one now.

In reality, it is even more important to use engagement letters with established clients and friends. Nothing will ruin a relationship faster than arguments over money. Don't allow miscommunication to destroy existing relationships with your clients. Use an engagement letter every single time. Don't let a legal dispute be the incentive you need to begin. Your engagement letter should always cover the type of work you will perform and the agreed-upon price. If there is a definite delivery date, include that, along with a clear message that the client must provide all the necessary paperwork by a given date in order to complete the work. A good rule of thumb is to also include a deadline for when work will be delivered to the client.

Many tax professionals also include deadlines for the client to follow. For example, you may want to indicate that any tax return that comes to you at the last minute may be automatically extended. The engagement letter can help prevent stress and prevent you from losing your mind.

Don't depend on verbal agreements to solidify your business relationships. The problem with verbal agreements is that the only record of the contract lies in the memory of each party. A verbal contract isn't worth the paper it's (not) written on. Unwritten promises are not easily enforceable and are a dangerous way to do business.

Example #1:

"Non-profit tax return will be ready for pick-up by May 1st. Any missing information not provided by _____ date will cause your tax return to be automatically extended."

Example #2:

"My fee for representation services will be based upon the amount of hours required at my standard billing rate of $125 per hour. Fees for representation will be billed as incurred. I require a retainer of $1,500 payable on acceptance of this agreement."

Include your payment terms. Consequences for late payment can include late fees or the right to stop services once a balance owed is past due. If the client knows your expectations BEFORE work begins, it will be much easier to collect your fees or end a working relationship, when necessary. Of course, if the client is in bankruptcy or owes large sums to the IRS, it goes without saying that you should demand a retainer before starting any work.

For your engagement letter to be valid, both parties must sign and date the agreement and each retain a copy of it. This indicates that there is a true meeting of the minds and that you both agree to the terms of the contract. There should be a statement to that effect just before the signature block of the document.

The next interview is with Darrell M. Carp, a highly experienced Enrolled Agent and a former IRS revenue officer. He will share his tips on how to attract lucrative clients and how to increase your client base by offering more IRS audit representation.

Interview with Darrell M. Carp, EA

Carp Tax Services, Inc.

www.carptaxservices.com

Professional Designations: Enrolled Agent, former IRS Senior Revenue Officer, former IRS Regional Analyst, Sustained Superior Performance awards from the IRS

Darrell, why don't you tell us a little about your practice.

Darrell: I started my practice in 1989 when I retired from the Internal Revenue Service. I was a Senior Revenue Officer. I then started my practice and I've been doing it for the last twenty years.

My first two years, I traveled around to people's homes and did taxes. I worked out of my home. After that, I got an office. You can do so much more once you have a permanent location.

At the beginning, what methods did you use to kick-start your practice?

Darrell: I generated my client base at the beginning through marketing. I used a service that mailed advertising to new homeowners in my area. It worked really well for me at the beginning.

The first year that I was in private practice, I did all of thirteen tax returns. I had retired from the IRS in the middle of March, so it was too late in the tax season to generate tax return clients. Nobody knew about my practice. After using the targeted advertising service for a few years, I went from a few returns to over 500 tax returns. It worked out really well—targeting the new homeowners. That's how I generated my income tax clients.

Then I didn't need the service anymore; my practice was just growing naturally through referrals, so I discontinued the service.

How do you generate new clients now?

Darrell: Well, currently my clients are all referrals. I haven't advertised anywhere in ten to twelve years. But I do maintain my website. My website always generates at least three to four new clients per year. The website only costs me $250 [per year]. So it's worth it.

Do you feel that your experience with the IRS gives you an advantage?

Darrell: Absolutely. The IRS didn't teach me a lot about taxes, if you can believe it. But the main reason why I have an advantage is in representation cases. For several years, most of the people I dealt with at the IRS were former co-workers of mine. It made it easier to negotiate things with people that I knew. This is one of the main reasons why my practice grew, through representation work. I had the advantage over other tax professionals because I knew how the IRS worked from the inside.

About a third of my practice is representation work and I do about 800 tax returns per year in addition to that. I use the interactive method with my clients. I meet with them for an hour; they're in, they're out, and they're done. I also use timesaving technology.

So much of your practice is IRS representation! That's unusual. Can you explain how you got so many representation clients?

Darrell: The representation side of my practice grew a lot from referrals. For some reason, people who owe money to the IRS always know other people who owe money to the IRS.

But I was also mass-mailing letters and my company information to people who had tax liens. When I first started out, I went down to the courthouse and collected names and addresses from people who had federal tax liens in excess of $10,000. Anything less than that wasn't worth it.

You have to find a way to generate more business. If you keep your tax practice a secret, you're going to go broke.

I noticed on your website that you talk about the IRS Offer in Compromise program (OIC Program). Do you see an increase in these clients?

Darrell: No, exactly the opposite. I've seen an extreme decrease in OIC offers, mainly because the government isn't really interested in doing offers anymore. Congress tacked on a $150 dollar application fee, which was mainly to discourage frivolous offers. I understand their position, but all it did was make the OIC program into a fundraiser.

Add that to the new requirement that the taxpayer has to submit 20 percent down upon submitting the offer (which is non-refundable under any circumstances) and it makes it impossible. The IRS is basically chasing people away from the OIC.

When you take on a representation case, do you require a retainer up-front?

Darrell: Yes, 100% of the time. You have to remember that these clients aren't paying their taxes. What makes you think they are going to pay their tax professional?

I required retainers from the very beginning. Look, whenever people talk to a lawyer, they always have to pay a retainer. With any professional who provides a service, customers generally have to pay some money up-front. So I simply follow the same guidelines.

And you do progress billing while the audit is taking place?

Darrell: Yes, if necessary.

How often do you go to IRS Appeals? Do you feel that you win more of your cases in appeals, rather than at the examination level?

Darrell: Well, tax professionals always win more concessions in appeals. Appeals are always easier, but they also consume more time. I'm never in any rush to go to appeals. I look at it this way—if I can wrap up the case quickly, then I can move onto the next case. My contract says that the retainer is mine to keep in any case, so the faster I can get the case resolved, the better.

I'm never anxious to go to appeals. I'm anxious to get the best deal for the client. I don't try to push things further just to try and increase the bill. I have plenty of work to keep me busy.

I also won't accept a tax case that I don't think I can win.

Oh, so you don't accept any tax protesters? {laughter}

Darrell: That's correct, I don't accept those cases.

However, I saw plenty of tax protesters when I was working for the IRS. Believe it or not, some of them actually had good points, but this is our tax system. We all have to live with it, and that's all there is to it.

Do you offer other tax and financial services? Like bookkeeping and payroll?

Darrell: I do some after-tax payroll, but that's about it. I have a lot of clients who have two to three employees, and they use QuickBooks to issue payroll checks. I use their QuickBooks file to issue the 941 forms and the New Jersey State payroll returns. It doesn't bring much money in—I just do it as a service to my clients.

The clients can't use the forms provided by QuickBooks because they are usually using the previous year's version and the forms have changed. Plus, the reporting requirements for the State of New Jersey are very confusing. With all the unemployment taxes, disability, and special forms—it's a lot of confusion. So, I just do it for the client. I don't charge much for payroll filings.

Do you have any other pointers that you would like to add that might help another tax preparer that was just starting out?

Darrell: Marketing. You just have to learn how to market yourself. There's a lot of competition from unlicensed preparers that you have to contend with. There are unlicensed preparers doing taxes out of their basement.

I have a funny real-life story about this. One day, I had a client come in with a horribly-prepared return. It was full of errors. I told the client (jokingly), "This looks like it was it was done in some guy's basement!" And he looked at me surprised and said, "How did you know?" I just couldn't believe it! The return was prepared by someone who was preparing taxes in his basement.

It's a matter of training. It's a matter of knowledge. So you have to market yourself—put yourself in a good position.

I would also suggest that new preparers try to get themselves a permanent "brick and mortar" location. It makes it easier for clients to find you and come to you.

Chapter 10

Inexpensive Marketing Techniques

"There is nothing wrong with a strategy to avoid the payment of taxes. The Internal Revenue Code doesn't prevent that."

-William H. Rehnquist, US Supreme Court Justice

Using Targeted Marketing and Newsletters

A lot of tax practitioners ignore the value of targeted advertising, which is often the most effective way to reach out to new clients. Of course, the best way to promote your tax services is to provide excellent service and quality. This will quickly become glowing "word-of-mouth" advertising for you. But how can you get new clients to come in and give your practice a try?

Traditional advertising, such as TV or radio ads, can be very expensive for a start-up practice. You don't have to spend thousands of dollars on advertising if you spend your money wisely.

Smart marketing is the key to success. Don't throw away opportunities to communicate with existing clients. In one form or another, customer communication may be the most vital marketing opportunity for a tax professional. Just like your employees, your clients need to know what is going on in the world of taxation. So, how do you communicate with them?

Enrolled Agents have an obligation to build relationships with their clients, and to let them know, with plenty of notice, every special "tax break" that might benefit them. The most effective way to do this is by collecting contact information from existing customers and building a customer database.

A customer database is made up of key facts about every customer who comes into your practice. The database should contain customers' first and last names, addresses, and phone and fax numbers whenever possible. E-mail addresses, telephone numbers, birthdays, and anniversaries are important if you want to send cards for special occasions.

It may also be helpful to know their favorite likes, dislikes, and the day the information was collected.

For some Enrolled Agents, spending marketing dollars on people who already know about their business seems like a waste of money, but your best advertising is your existing customer base.

Don't let them forget you, so they will always know who to recommend whenever a family member or a friend has a tax question they can't answer.

Keep yourself in your clients' minds at all times. There will always be opportunities for them to recommend you to someone else. Don't ever pass up the chance to remind your clients that you offer a wide range of consulting and financial services, and that they can come to you for advice outside the regular tax season.

Newsletter Marketing

Andrew Johnson, EA decides to start a monthly e-mail newsletter called *"Johnson's Tax Tips."* Andrew's long-time client, Jennie Jones, reads about the fantastic education credits available for college tuition. Jennie doesn't have any kids, but her nephew Tommy is about to start school and Jennie's brother-in-law just mentioned how expensive the tuition costs were and how he *wished* he could talk to someone about his options.

Jennie immediately remembers Andrew's e-mail and forwards it to her brother-in-law, who calls up and schedules an appointment.

Voilà! Another great referral.

Support People Who Support You!

Don't advertise in the Yellow Pages or use expensive magazine ads for useless print advertising. A single Yellow Page ad can cost thousands of dollars. For the same amount of money, you can run thousands of advertisements on the Internet. Very few people use phone books these days. Almost everyone goes to the Internet to look up a telephone number or a business. I can attest to this—I use my iPhone for everything. I have not opened a phone book in years.

If you decide to do any print advertising, market locally, and support your own clients. When your existing clients approach you to advertise in their high school yearbook, church newsletter, or county fair flier, then do it. Save your valuable marketing dollars and support those in your community who support you.

Support your loyal customers by circulating community dollars back into the community. Advertising with local businesses also raises your community profile.

This is especially helpful if you have contacts within a certain ethnic or religious group, such as the Russian community, the disabled community, or even the local Catholic Church. These are all examples of "niche markets."

You can target a niche market simply by being a visible member of that community. Shake hands. Get to know people. Mention your business. Give free advice at local gatherings. People love to hear how they can lower their taxes. Once again, always make sure you have your business card handy.

Advertising is crucial to gaining exposure for your tax practice, but you don't have to spend a fortune to drive business to your door. Try to think of more creative ways to promote your business locally without spending a lot of money.

The next interview is with Bill Fulcher, EA MBA, who has a long-running practice in Texas. He has been a successful EA for more than forty years and jump-started his tax practice very successfully by using targeted mail techniques before e-mail even existed! Although bulk mail is not an effective advertising method, targeted mailings are very effective. Don't try to reach everybody.

Bill supplements his income from tax preparation by offering additional services, such as insurance and securities, as he is also licensed as a securities dealer and insurance agent. His office offers bookkeeping, tax preparation, and a full range of financial services. He also does a fair number of out-of-state returns.

Interview with Bill Fulcher, EA MBA

www.billfulcher.com

Professional Designations: Enrolled Agent, Master of Business Administration (MBA)

Can you tell me a little bit about your practice?

Bill: Yes, I have an active tax practice in Texas. My ex-wife was a professional bookkeeper, and I got interested in the tax and bookkeeping business because of her.

I was helping her out in her bookkeeping business, and during the tax season, I just kept helping her more and more. So after two years of part-time practice I went full-time.

I got a student loan to go back to school and got my education. The first few years were tough, and we just had to tighten our belts.

We found a nice office in town and the owner allowed us to rent it really cheap. So that was our first "official" office.

Did you do any advertising to generate business at the beginning?

Bill: At the very beginning, we went out and pulled the voter registration list for our precinct. The list had lots of names and addresses. The list was just for a very small area, but it still had about 3,000 names and addresses on it.

So we sat down and wrote each one of those voters a letter and told them we would be happy to do their tax returns. We wrote these letters before the tax season began. By golly, they just started coming in.

You're the first Enrolled Agent that I've spoken to that has used this resource. How did you get the list?

Bill: I paid a small fee at the courthouse and got the list. It's public information. I only did it the first few years. Then we started generating referrals, and clients started recommending us to their friends. We advertised in the local newspaper a lot, too, but none of the print advertising was as effective as the individual letters.

I took an advertising course in school and my instructor told me that he had seen the ad for my tax practice in the paper. So I know people noticed the ad, but I could never figure out how effective the newspaper ads were at actually bringing in new clients.

Word-of-mouth advertising is really the best. But you need something to get started. I felt the voter registration list and letter were very effective at the beginning.

So you don't believe that print advertising is very effective?

I've done a lot of print advertising, and I'm not very happy with the return. But the most effective print advertising I've ever done didn't even have my name on it. I ran an ad that said:

"What your tax preparer doesn't want you to know... he or she is **not licensed**... *unless he or she is an Enrolled Agent, CPA, or attorney at law."*

That ad was the most effective print advertising I've ever done. And I just put my telephone number on it. I got a lot of response from that one.

I saw from your website that you do a lot of out-of-state returns. How do you generate out-of-state clients?

Bill: I do have clients all over the United States. And it's because, generally, my clients stay with me when they move away. I do lots of out-of-state returns because I make it easy for clients to reach me even after they move away.

People send me their tax information from all over—they want to keep using me as their preparer even after they've moved away.

That says something about your clients' loyalty.

Bill: Yes, I guess it does.

Do you offer additional services besides tax preparation?

Bill: Yes, we offer bookkeeping and always have. But I specialize mostly in taxation and IRS Appeals.

About 90 percent of my business is tax, with the remaining amount from other services.

Do you mainly focus on individual returns?

Bill: Yes, we have a few small businesses accounts and a large business client on South Padre Island that has a business in Mexico. But most of our returns and appeals are individuals.

Chapter 11

Targeting Niche Markets

"The ancient Egyptians built elaborate fortresses and tunnels and even posted guards at tombs to stop grave robbers. In today's America, we call that *estate planning.*"

-Bill Archer

The Benefits of "Niche" Marketing

The following interview is with David Hatt, a highly successful Enrolled Agent in Menlo Park, California. A former president of the NAEA, David participates in many professional organizations.

David also understands how to target a "niche" market. David earned a Master's degree in taxation. His Master's thesis was on the taxation of domestic partners. This made him an instant expert in one of the most complex (and misunderstood) areas of taxation. Because of his specialized expertise, David successfully markets to the gay community. In California, this is a source of many high-end clients, who are usually too confused by domestic partnership laws to attempt their own tax returns. David also specializes in complex stock transactions.

Do you have a "niche" market that you can target? You can decide to specialize in a vast number of different industries. There are special skill areas that you can hone in order to market directly to a specific group in your community.

Perhaps you speak fluent Japanese or you have contacts in the deaf community. Maybe you have experience in estates, non-taxable exchanges, or the taxation of clergy members. Construction and manufacturing are two niche markets that are highly lucrative. Many tax professionals pursue special training in these areas.

The US tax system is so complex that no one can possibly be an "expert" at everything. Add to that the complexity of state income taxes and it is no wonder that taxpayers tear their hair out trying to comply with the law, much less understand it! The key is to specialize.

Find a group or particular area of tax law that you enjoy and start marketing to that niche.

The benefits of niche marketing are many:

1. You're the Expert
You set yourself up as an "expert" in one particular sensitive area of taxation, which will generate multiple referrals from others in the community with the same unique problem.

2. Less Price Shopping
People are less likely to argue about the price of your services if they perceive you to be an expert in one particular area of taxation. You can handle this by calmly having a "take-it-or-leave-it" attitude when potential clients quibble about price. They will usually pipe down when they see that you are serious about the level of your expertise.

Engagement letters are particularly effective in this respect. Give the client a clear listing and breakdown of your fees. Once they see the complexity of the work you do in writing, they are likely to agree to the engagement.

3. Easier to Advertise
A niche client is easier to find and easier to advertise to. In many cases, the client will be looking for a professional that will address their particular tax situation. That means *they* are looking for *you*, rather than the other way around.

Interview with David Hatt, EA MS

www.davidhattea.com

Professional Designations: Enrolled Agent, Master's in Taxation, Former President of the National Association of Enrolled Agents (NAEA), Graduate Fellow of NTPI

How did you get started in this business?

David: I was employed as an accountant. After five years, I was still making the same salary. I was good with numbers, and I wanted to make more money. So I took an H&R Block tax preparation course. I thought it was fun.

Then I interviewed with H&R Block and was hired on. They usually give tax preparers a commission in addition to their regular wage. So the harder you work, the more money you make. When I interviewed, the supervisor at H&R told me that first-year preparers usually don't earn a bonus commission… so I worked *my tail off*. I got a big bonus my first year. I realized that the harder I worked, the smarter I got, and the more money I made.

I learned how to interview people, talk to them, and answer questions. In 1992, I worked for H&R Block during the entire tax season. That summer, I found out about the Enrolled Agent exam. There were already two EAs in the H&R Block office, and they told me about it.

H&R Block had a back room with a study guide, so I started looking at the study questions for the EA exam. I thought, "These questions are hard! I'm never going to be able to answer these!" But as time went on, I started learning more and more.

I soon realized that there was no drawback to actually taking the test, so I spent the entire summer studying for it. I took an EA course offered through the Golden Gate chapter of the California Society of Enrolled Agents. I took H&R Block's tax education class at night, too. I studied and studied.

I passed all four parts[31] of the exam on my first try. I got my exam results in December 1992.

In 1993, the other Enrolled Agents in the H&R Block office left, and all three of us opened an office together in Menlo Park, California. We've been together ever since.

So you're not partners, you just share an office?

David: Right, so we really get the best of both worlds. We divide the rent by one-third, and we divide the cost of our tax software. We get to bounce ideas off each other, and we help each other out. We make appointments for each other when one of us is gone.

A lot of preparers strike out on their own; do you think it's more difficult?

David: It is harder. It's so much more expensive.

At the beginning, we shared one printer. I'll never forget that printer! It only carried about fifty sheets of paper—if you can imagine trying to print tax returns. It was networked, but only one of us could print a return at once. It would get jammed all the time and we'd have to re-set it. It was a lot of fun {laughter}.

Of course, we each have our own printer now.

So you felt that your experience with H&R Block gave you the experience you needed to start your own practice?

David: Yes, I did. I remember—I got my enrollment card on December 30th, 1992. On December 31st (one day later), I went to my boss and quit. I had to.

Really? That was brave.

David: Yes, I thought, "It's *now or never.*" It was a leap of faith. That season, (in 1993) I worked for a CPA firm in Sunnyvale. I worked in a back room. I reviewed tax returns. I learned how to check tax returns for accuracy. In the CPA office, I learned how to verify returns and get experience with harder problems.

With H&R Block, you have a lot of customers off the street. So *that* experience taught me how to talk to people and do client interviews.

I also went back to school to earn my Master's in Taxation. Having the Master's degree helped me out a lot. The Master's gave me a good background, because the basic concepts don't change. Tax law changes from year to year, but the basics pretty much stay the same.

One class was all about the IRS appeals process. The same week I started the class, I had a client who needed to file an IRS appeal. I told her what I felt we could appeal successfully, and which areas I thought we might lose. Sure enough, I was right.

Now, when you left H&R Block, what did you do to kick-start your client base?

David: Well, it's unethical to steal clients from former employers. We did not contact any former clients. We advertised in all the local newspapers and the Country Almanac. We placed large photos of ourselves in the advertisements. So clients saw our photos, and **they** called **us**.

What a great idea! Then the clients could find you based on your photograph.

David: Yes. They recognized our pictures, and it gave them a way to make their own choice whether or not to call us.

Do you have any particular type of advertising that you felt was more effective?

David: I advertised in the Gay and Lesbian newspapers, and also the *OutNow Directory*, which is a gay-friendly directory. You don't have to be gay to place an ad. I got a lot of referrals from those ads. I also advertised in a directory called the *Lavender Pages* which was like a Yellow Pages for gay-friendly businesses. I got a lot of high-end clients from that.

So you actively targeted a niche market, the gay and lesbian community?

David: Yes, and it worked. Really—my best advertising are my existing clients. Now all of my referrals are word-of-mouth.

We stopped advertising about a year ago, although we still are listed in the Yellow Pages. We stopped the rest of the advertising because we have enough business as it is. I tried to develop a boutique practice. I want to stay busy, but still have time to devote to my existing clientele.

Regarding pricing, my advice is that you want people to go to you because you are good, not because you are cheap. Because once you start raising your prices, those clients will bolt.

I had another EA tell me once, "Fifty-dollar clients refer *other* fifty-dollar clients. Thousand-dollar clients will refer *other* thousand-dollar clients." So you have to determine what type of practice you want to have. If you have problem clients, they will give their "problem" friends to you.

Do you target a particular tax specialty, as well?

David: Yes, I have extensive knowledge of domestic partnerships, on which I did my Master's thesis. I also specialize in stock options. This is Silicon Valley. So I'm a whiz at tax planning for stock options.

With incentive stock options, you have the bargain element, which is the difference between the FMV on the date of exercise minus the exercise price. That bargain element isn't taxed under normal tax rules. It's taxed under AMT. So people have to pay the higher of the two: either regular income tax or AMT. So I tell people to look at their options.

It takes a lot of tax planning to do it right. For example, in some cases, I would tell clients to exercise options early in the year, say, before April 1st. So the following year, they would have a huge AMT tax to pay. But then they sell the stock on April 3rd, and that way they get a credit, so the following year we can get their tax down to zero. It's complex and every client has different needs.

So you do tax planning throughout the year?

David: Yes, absolutely, especially with some of the bigger clients. We meet and discuss their tax situation. I work all year round. There's plenty of work for me to do. But I still make time to volunteer for my professional associations.

Do you do a lot of representation?

David: No. That's one trapeze I don't reach for. It's time consuming, and it's unpleasant. I'd rather focus on tax preparation and planning.

If the audit case is an existing client, I always take it on because I have the records. I don't take an adversarial position with the IRS. I just consider it to be a situation where the IRS wants to see proof of something. So I provide it. I try to calm my clients during the audit process. I tell them that they haven't done anything wrong, but that they just need to provide proof.

As for new representation cases, I usually refer those to other Enrolled Agents who specialize in representation. I know what I'm good at.

Do you offer ancillary services, such as payroll or bookkeeping?

David: No, no. I have one payroll account as a favor to a client. But otherwise, no. There are bookkeepers out there that prepare payroll. I'd rather focus on tax preparation and tax planning.

Which tax software do you use?

David: Lacerte.

Do you feel like this is a bad time to start a tax practice?

David: No, the best part about being self-employed is that you don't have to worry about getting laid off. I have so many clients with sad stories about getting laid off. My income has been affected by the economy, but I always have a positive cash flow. At least I have income. People always have to have their taxes prepared.

I see that you've done radio and television interviews. How do you get that kind of press exposure?

David: I'm really involved in the EA community. Last year, I was the President of the NAEA. I was on **The Today Show** *twice.* At the end of tax season, they asked for eight Enrolled Agents to answer tax questions from viewers. So I was on a phone bank, and it was fun. I got to fly to New York and answer all these tax questions from the audience. It was fun to do.

So you stay active in all your professional organizations? Does your involvement lift your community profile, or does it generate more clients?

David: Yes, for me, I was involved from day one, ever since I got my Treasury card. I went to my first chapter meeting just five days later.

In the past five years, I've had three Enrolled Agents contact me *first* when they put their practices up for sale. They were going to retire, and they knew how hard I worked for my clients, and they thought it would be a good fit.

They knew me. This is because I had lunch with them and dinner with them, and we knew each other through our professional memberships.

Did you purchase those tax practices?

David: Yes, I did! All three.

What is the make-up of your client base? Do you do a lot of business returns?

David: Currently, I do about twenty Partnership and Corporate returns, and the rest are individual tax returns.

What advice do you have for EAs that are just starting out?

David: You have to treat each client like they are part of your family. Be friendly. Be warm, and above all, be *responsive!* Don't ever let your clients feel like they are a "problem" for you.

Respond to clients. Always respond. Sometimes you get e-mails or calls from clients, and you don't have the time to research something, but always make sure you call. Return their call, and tell the client that you are busy, but that you haven't forgotten their problem. Give them a time frame for when you can get them the answer they need. People don't mind waiting, but they hate being ignored.

And new preparers should get involved. I built my tax practice with information that I've gotten from other tax professionals. Go to events. Go to dinners. I learned a lot. I incorporated those good tips into my own tax practice, and it was all free advice. You can learn information from other EAs that can help you build and promote your practice.

Chapter 12

Local Media and Free Publicity

"Give your business the *best chance* of being covered by the local news media… give them what they are looking for."

-SCORE

Using Local Media

Our next interview is with Kristin Delfau, an author and Enrolled Agent in Connecticut. She has a highly successful home-based practice. Kristin has developed a niche practice that offers tax advice and planning to individuals, many of whom are referrals from legal professionals.

Kristin actively promotes her business regionally by using local media. As a published author, she uses her writing to get free publicity from local newspapers. She contacts editors with ideas for articles. If her idea is accepted, she gets her article printed in the newspaper, along with a byline and her contact information. This way, she gets her picture and business information in the newspaper without having to pay for advertising.

She is a contributor to many magazines and publications, including NATP's *TAXPRO Monthly.* In addition to her published articles, Kristin is also the author of the book *Turbo-Mom's Guide to Saving Money Without Wasting Time,* which is a common sense book about personal finance targeted to busy moms. All of this publicity boosts her community profile and increases her credibility.

A quick search on Google for "Kristin Delfau, EA" comes up with over 50,000 web hits. Her articles and interviews are everywhere—and not just in tax publications. She has articles at *Voice Over Xtra* (a voice-over company), *Investor Blogger,* and *Blog Talk Radio.*

The best part of all of these articles and interviews is that they generate more web traffic and publicity for her tax practice. Kristin is an Enrolled Agent who knows how to publicize her business!

She also does live interviews for radio and television; she makes herself available as the "local expert" in taxes.

Remember: advertising costs money, but *publicity* is free.

Referrals from Mediators

Kristin's practice also includes a number of referrals from divorce mediators and other legal professionals. In order to get these referrals, she deliberately contacted divorce mediators in her area and offered consulting services.

Her practice offers formal *Divorce Agreement Review*, which is a service in which she offers structured tax advice for people going through a divorce. Knowing (as many of us do) that divorce attorneys are often ignorant of the tax consequences of divorce agreements, Kristin has built a large following based on her extensive knowledge of this niche market.

She offers year-round tax planning and other financial services to individuals only (no business entities). Kristin has decided to focus her highly successful boutique practice on individual taxation. This method has worked well for her and allows her to focus all her energies on a niche market.

If a client comes to her and wants to form a corporation, she refers him or her to a colleague in her professional networking group. In return, many of these tax professionals refer back to her when they have a question about the tax consequences of a divorce or would like an honest opinion about their clients' life insurance policies.

Can you think of any professionals in your neighborhood who might need your services? Think about it. Legal referrals can be highly lucrative if you know how to get them.

Interview with Kristin Delfau, EA, MA

Delfau Tax & Financial Services

www.delfautax.com

Author: Turbo-Mom's Guide to Saving Money Without Wasting Time

Professional Designations: Enrolled Agent, Master of Arts (MA), Financial Planner, Fulbright scholar, published author

Can you tell us about how you started in this business?

Kristin: After studying and working abroad, I came back to the United States and ended up working for an independent tax preparation and financial services firm. I was initially recruited to work as a financial planner. My new employer insisted that everyone working in the office take a basic tax course. I wasn't thrilled about it, but I ended up loving the tax work. Then I started working more and more on the tax side. When I had my son, I decided to open my own firm.

When did you decide to publish a book on personal finance?

Kristin: I was always the person that people came to when they were looking for information about a bargain. I was also seeing in the financial world how women were treated.

I wanted to help women get a better grasp on their finances, so they aren't made to feel stupid. Just because a woman might not know what questions to ask—that doesn't make her stupid.

This was intended to give women a fun but informative Q&A-style reference guide so that they could take better control of their financial lives.

I had this idea for a book, and I ended up finding a publisher by accident. My publisher liked my book proposal. I ended up with a publishing contract, and I wrote the book after I had my son. I designed the book for mothers who don't have a lot of time or money to waste.

How did you generate clients at the beginning?

Kristin: At the beginning, I had referrals from existing clients as well as local attorneys with whom I've worked in the past and who like my flat fee approach. I've gotten clients through a Craigslist ad (*www.craigslist.org*). I've even picked up clients from other tax professionals because I do a lot of multi-state returns. I like referrals the best. I want a certain type of client. A tax professional doesn't want to have 300 clients that all want to file on October 15th.

I've found clients at my book talks and also through my networking group, BNI. If you join the group and offer helpful suggestions, you will get referrals from the group.

What exactly is BNI?

Kristin: BNI (Business Networking International) is the largest business networking organization in the world.[32] It's a networking group and everyone in the organization is looking to promote their business. The organization will only allow one person *per profession* into the chapter, so you aren't competing with other tax pros.

How about local business groups?

Kristin: I would encourage new preparers to join their local *Chamber of Commerce*, too. You can often get discounts on health insurance and it's a good networking opportunity.

You've decided to post your pricing right on your website. Describe your practice model, because it's different than what we usually see.

Kristin: I'm not trying to build an empire. I have a family, and that's more important than anything else. My practice is different because I'm very selective about the clients I choose to work with.

I bill on a flat fee basis. I'm not the cheapest in town, but I'm certainly not the most expensive. In my location, my prices are average. My base rates are right on my website. But I have very little overhead, which mostly consists of my software and supply costs. I am a sole practitioner, and I have a very professional home office.

I also try to be as technologically advanced as possible so I can keep my costs down. For example, I use a VOIP[33] phone line. It costs me $10 per month, and I have unlimited long-distance calling. I can call anywhere in the country.

My office is paperless. I'm not printing out tons of returns and wasting reams and reams of paper. By streamlining, I can keep my costs lower and save time. This saves the client money as well.

Can you explain your "flat fee" billing?

Kristin: I'm very up-front about my costs, which clients appreciate. Most of my clients are middle income or high income. I'm pretty cognizant of how much time it takes me to prepare a return. Clients know that if I quote them $300 or $550—that is what they are going to pay. Each client signs a letter agreeing to the fee beforehand.

I do allow some room for negotiation if the client doesn't disclose everything, like, "Oh, by the way, I have three rental apartments." I have to protect myself in that regard.

But I build a certain level of trust with my clients, and they appreciate that I'm straightforward. I also bill a flat fee for tax research. If a client comes to me with a complicated problem, I'll let them know how much it will cost and if it seems worth it to them to have a well-researched answer, they will pay it. They have the option to decline. They decide. I've never had anyone decline.

I put it all on the table. There's no surprises in flat fee billing.

For example, in other tax practices, a client might bring in a tax return that usually costs them $300, and let's say this year there's a complicated problem. The return fee goes from $300 to $750, which no one told them about, plus the taxpayer might owe a large sum to the IRS and/or the state. Clients *hate* that. I hate it when my plumber does it to me, and it's no different when doing someone's tax return.

Clients don't mind paying your fee if they know what to expect, but they don't like surprises.

You're the first EA that I've spoken to that bills on a flat fee structure. What do you do in the cases of IRS representation or audit work?

Kristin: I refer representation cases and OIC cases out to another Enrolled Agent who specializes in those cases. That's not the focus of my practice. I do planning and personal income tax. I also do divorce agreement review as well as insurance services for individuals. I think that it's expensive and complicated if you try to do ***everything***. You can't be everything to everyone.

It's good to develop a niche. Find an angle. Don't try to be everything to everybody because you will end up being good at nothing.

For example, if you enjoy doing rentals or 1031 exchanges, get involved in some real estate networking groups. The brokers and real estate agents will know who's buying, and they will refer them to you. Get your name out there.

If you like doing estate tax returns, start talking to funeral directors. It sounds morbid, but it's true. If you really enjoy estate taxation, you shouldn't be talking to 30 year olds. Go give talks at 55-plus communities. Get a piece of your marketing material at a local funeral home.

You have to think outside the box. Try to go where the other tax preparers *aren't*. You have to test-market yourself.

What is the demographic of your client base?

Kristin: I don't do business entities, because I have decided to specialize in individuals. I do tax planning and research throughout the year. I do cash flow, budgeting, debt payoff planning, etc. for my clients who want it. I will do an integrated financial plan for people, for which I charge a flat fee that could range anywhere from $750 to $3,000, depending on the complexity of the situation. I was licensed in the securities arena for five years, but I have eschewed that in order to focus on my tax practice.

No matter what service I am providing to clients, I explain all the reasons for my recommendations. I teach people how to work through their debts.

Whenever I do a plan, I disclose everything in writing. I see the biggest problem in financial services in general is that clients never seem to know who is getting paid to do what. I want my clients to know why I am providing the advice I am providing them.

Can you explain the Divorce Agreement Review services that you offer?

Kristin: Divorce Agreement Review is something that is close to my heart. I get referrals from divorce mediators. I look over the agreements and adjust the language so that the agreement conforms to tax code as well as clarifies items that are too vague and could lead to problems down the road.
Often, the divorce attorneys are not fully versed in tax law. I give advice on how to deal with trickier aspects of taxes, like when there are stock options involved.

Often, I can prevent problems before they occur, and usually one of the spouses becomes a client.

This is why I try to keep my practice focused. I am very choosy about the client that I will agree to take.

How did you initially generate the referrals from divorce mediators?

Kristin: I just introduced myself and cold-called. I made an appointment with the mediator.

I'm not actively trying to obtain referrals from *litigating* divorce attorneys, because those divorces are usually too messy. I like divorce mediators because these are usually couples who are trying to resolve their issues without fighting.

There's always a modicum of tension, of course. But it's a lot more amicable because the people are trying to sort these issues out properly.

An EA can help the process along. By sorting out a potentially thorny tax problem, I usually end up helping both spouses in a positive way.

How did you obtain your EA license? Did you take the EA exam or did you work for the IRS?

Kristin: I took the Enrolled Agent exam.

Do you do any advertising?

Kristin: Not traditional advertising. I have a website. But I actually get free advertising because I work with the local press. I shoot the editor ideas for different story topics. I have a contact at my local paper, and sometimes I get a write-up. The paper will do a full story and I get my picture in the paper. I don't feel that print ads or ads in phone books have enough of a return to justify the investment.

Have you ever done any advertising and felt that it was a waste of money?

Kristin: Yes, I've done print advertising in the local paper, and I've used mass-mailing. It just wasn't targeted enough. My marketing needs to be targeted because I am looking for a certain type of client. I've also done some radio interviews.

Radio interviews! That's the best kind of press—free press.

Kristin: Yes, I like doing interviews because it builds my credibility.

What software do you use?

Kristin: I use Ultra Tax CS. My advice to new preparers is to keep their business costs low, but not to skimp on their software. Don't try to do all your tax returns on TurboTax the first year and force people to paper-file. Pay the money for good software and save costs elsewhere.

Ultra Tax is pricey. Lacerte is not immune to that, either. At the beginning, you can purchase a limited license and pay per filed return. You can just pay as you go. When you get big enough, then you can invest in the unlimited license.

Honestly, clients don't care what kind of folder you use and if it is embossed or not. They DO care if you screwed up on their return because you went cheap on your software and your software could not calculate their return properly.

Any advice on pricing?

Kristin: Don't under-price yourself. It's one of the first things I learned. If you try to compete with H&R Block, you are always going to lose and you won't attract good clients. You'll only attract people who are *price*-shopping. They are not *quality*-shopping.

How about office staff?

Kristin: Preparers shouldn't feel pressured to employ office staff at the beginning. Just grow organically.

Get a good client-contact system. You need to be able to keep track of your clients. I like *Advisors Assistant.* It's a client management system for people in the Financial Services industries.[34] It basically keeps track of all your clients' information, investments, mailing lists, insurance, etc.

If you are a financial planner as well as a tax preparer, it's a great way to keep track of client information all in one place.

Do you have any specific advice for Enrolled Agents that are just starting out?

Kristin: I advise them to join worthwhile organizations. Find a good local support network. We have a local organization—*New York/Connecticut Association of Tax Professionals.* It's such a great local organization. We all lean on each other for ideas and advice.

We aren't competing with each other. There are enough tax clients to go around. The older tax professionals can help the younger ones with the tax knowledge, and the younger members can help older preparers with their technology hurdles. Also, many established preparers receive more referrals than they can handle. If you can build a solid relationship with a preparer or two of this type, they might have an arrangement with you where they will send those referrals on to you.

You should also join a national organization like NATP. Professional tax organizations are a great way to connect with people. And the membership fee is a lot cheaper than traditional advertising.

Also, find two to three networking organizations in your area, such as the BNI group as mentioned earlier or an active Chamber of Commerce. Once you discover your niche market, find a group that supports that niche.

Finally, contact your local branch of the SBDC (a division of the SBA), which is usually located on college campuses in your area. It is a free service through the SBA with paid advisors who will help you design a business and marketing plan so that you can better define your goals and reach them.

Chapter 13

Marketing to Expatriates

"The two most important words whenever a client provides you with a referral are *thank you.* Even if a prospect never becomes a client, don't forget to say *thank you* to both the prospect and the person providing the referral."

- AICPA: The American Institute of Certified Public Accountants

Expatriate Returns

Doing tax returns for US residents and non-residents living abroad can be a rewarding business. With the IRS Offshore Voluntary Disclosure Program, many people are looking specifically for tax professionals who have experience with foreign-earned income and foreign bank accounts.

If you choose to specialize in this complex area of income taxation, expect to be rewarded with clients who are generally high-income. These clients usually don't quibble over fees.

Since they live overseas, they will typically mail or e-mail documents to you, which means that you save precious face-to-face time. Most of your questions can be handled via e-mail, which is easier and safer for you, since you have a written record of all your communications with the client. Perhaps you believe that getting these clients is too difficult—but a quick Google search brings up dozens of tax professionals who specialize in expatriate returns.

Getting these lucrative clients can be as easy as setting up a website and paying for Google AdWords. Advertising online is easy! Every time a potential client searches for "expatriate taxes," your website can be featured. It's a small investment for a big return.

With Google AdWords, you only pay when someone actually "clicks" on your ad. AdWords has been a very lucrative referral source for me, and the cost is minimal—less than $200 a month. It can be adjusted to fit your budget, too. You can spend as little or as much as you want.

You can offer expatriate tax preparation and consulting services for US citizens working abroad and foreign nationals. You can also offer tax return preparation for non-residents who have a filing requirement. For example, potential clients could include foreign investors, musicians, authors, or other foreign persons who have taxable income from US sources and currently are living overseas.

The best part of this market is—once you *start* servicing these clients, you start getting word-of-mouth referrals almost immediately. That's because expatriates usually live and work with other expatriates.

Clients will appreciate it if you provide innovative tax planning, consulting, and expatriate tax tips that help them legally reduce their tax liability. Foreign tax treaties are a muddy area, but you can always specialize in one country, and limit your risk.

Interview with Chet Burgess, EA

Brookwood Tax Service

www.brookwoodtax.com

Professional Designations: Enrolled Agent, President of the Georgia NAEA

Chet Burgess is an Enrolled Agent practicing in Georgia. So, how long have you been practicing, and how did you get started in this business?

Chet: I was a journalist for thirty years and worked for CNN. I was a reporter and anchor in Virginia. I then became an executive producer, and managed the CNN newsroom for a number of years. When CNN and America Online merged, I decided it might be a good time for a career change.

I've always been interested in personal finance. I started doing my own tax returns on a personal computer. Years ago, I sold some insurance and mutual funds. I did it part-time, but I didn't enjoy it, because of the sales aspect. I've been an avid reader of the Wall Street Journal for years, as well as a number of other finance magazines. I felt that I was pretty well-informed when I made the decision to give tax accounting a try.

How did you get your initial tax training?

Chet: I took the route that many people take: I took the H&R Block tax course. I worked for H&R Block for one tax season. I loved working with people and untangling tax problems. But I hated H&R Block's marketing tactics. I decided right away that I needed to get a license and set out my own shingle.

Did you start your business from scratch after that first season with H&R Block?

Chet: Yes, I work successfully from a home office. My business is a home-based business. As soon as I finished my first tax season with Block, I ordered an EA study course. I studied from May 1st to the end of September, and I passed the EA exam the first time, all four parts. I passed the EA exam in 2002.

That following January, I set up my website, set out my shingle, and off I went.

So you enjoy working from home?

Chet: I would never go back to a storefront.

When they start out, a lot of EAs will take any client that walks through the door.

Chet: When you're new in business, you'll take anyone who can "fog a mirror." If a client can breathe, they're in! But having that [mentality] is a mistake.

How did you advertise in the beginning?

Chet: I placed advertisements in a small neighborhood newspaper the first year. I bought a mailing list of 5,000 households. All of that advertising generated only three referrals. So I never used print advertising again.

The website has been a good source of referrals. Right now, I don't pay for any web advertising. I just pay for my domain. I've done my own search engine optimization, which varies in effectiveness.

But for the first five years, I generated the most referrals from a business networking group. There is a regional group in Atlanta called Powercore (*www.powercore.net*), which I joined. There is also a similar national group called BNI, or Business Networking International.

Can you tell us a little more about the group?

Chet: Yes, I joined Powercore because you meet with the same group of professionals, usually from about fifteen to twenty-five people. You get to know each others' businesses very well. I still have a lot of those relationships. One of them is a small-business attorney. He still handles all of my legal needs. I refer clients to him, and he refers clients to me.

For a five-year period, while I was part of this group, three-quarters of my client base came from either direct or indirect referrals from Powercore.

Now I don't do any networking. With the exception of the website, I don't advertise. I am at a point where I feel comfortable with the number of clients I have. I'm pretty busy year-round. Even after October 15, I have amended returns or stragglers that I have to deal with.

For example, right now I am working on a **Form 1045** for a client. They had business losses that we are going to carry back. They will get a nice refund from that.

So you work all year round?

Chet: I do, but not full-time. In the middle of the summer and in November after things settle down, I work only about half time. I'll take a few days off during the week. But I still check voicemail and e-mail every day.

On your website, it says that you specialize in the *Foreign Earned Income Exclusion.* Do you do a lot of these types of returns? Is this a niche market that you have discovered?

Chet: Yes, that is one of my specialties. I started doing these returns entirely by accident. In 2003, I received an e-mail inquiry from a potential client, who was working as a network administrator in the Middle East.

This client had just found my website, and she decided to contact me. She had contacted four other tax preparers, two of whom are CPAs. She received four different answers.

When I got the e-mail, I was on a ski trip. It was early January, and I was taking a little vacation just before I got busy. During the ski trip, I took half a day to do research on her specific situation, and I sent her a two-page response.

The client liked what I had to say, and she became my first overseas client. Since then, I've picked up many others, both from my website and also from referrals.

Do you target other niche markets?

Chet: Yes, in fact, I am working on a few returns right now for real estate agents. These are cascading amended returns; they are all real estate agents or mortgage brokers that have multiple foreclosures (investment properties). They got caught up in the crash.

In fact, most of my foreclosures are from clients that actually worked in the housing industry. In some cases, these clients had great difficulty getting records together.

Multiple banks and title companies have closed—how do you handle those situations?

Chet: In most cases, we file with the best information available. Later, sometimes we get more precise information from the lender. Congress added changes to the law regarding forgiving debt.

I have three clients who were able to exclude debt cancellation income because they were insolvent. The IRS is backlogged with amended returns, so I have been watching IRS e-services to see when the original returns are accepted so I can file amendments.

So this is the type of work you do throughout the year? You charge the client for the amended return or any NOL carryback?

Chet: Absolutely. Unless it's a mistake that I made. I just did an amended return for a long-term client who got caught in the real estate crunch. He purchased two beachfront properties at the height of the market. He ended up having to short sale one property, and he still has the other one. The home is a vacation rental, and part of the mortgage interest was disallowed, and I neglected to carry over the disallowed portion to **Schedule A.** So I did the amended return at no charge.

But, for the most part, I charge market rates for amended returns.

You also do representation work. How much of your practice is IRS representation?

Chet: About 10 to 15 percent of my practice is representation work. I usually do representation for my existing clients. The first couple of years I was in practice, I did quite a few multi-year delinquent filers. But I discovered that chronic tax procrastinators *continue to be* chronic procrastinators. Only about 20 percent of those people turned into in good, long-term clients.

I don't deal with the tax "disasters" anymore. You know— those clients that ignored the IRS for five years and have received the *final notice of intent to levy.* If they come to me and their bank accounts have already been seized, I refer them to someone else. I have an acquaintance who is a retired collections officer, I send those clients to her. These clients are "past the tourniquet stage."

Representation can be very lucrative. I know a handful of EAs who specialize in representation, and they charge very nice fees. They get retainers up-front, so if the client decides to disappear, their money is in the bank.

But I like to sleep at night. I don't enjoy high tension confrontations or deadlines. I don't want to deal with a revenue officer who wants a completed Form 433-A filed by next Monday. I just don't want that kind of pressure.

What is the client make-up of your practice?

Chet: I do roughly 30 percent small business, mostly LLCs and S-Corps. The rest are individual clients.

Do you get referrals from other professionals?

Chet: I have a relationship with a bilingual bookkeeper who works with the Hispanic population of Atlanta. She attended a tax course that I taught a few years ago. She approached me after the course was over and asked if she could refer her corporate tax returns to me. It's worked out very well. I've helped a number of her clients obtain ITINs and I've learned a little Spanish in the process.

Do you offer bookkeeping or insurance?

Chet: I don't do bookkeeping or payroll. I refer those out. I'm strictly a tax practitioner. I think that insurance and securities are so fraught with conflicts of interest that I've never offered those products. The first two years I was in business I offered a type of RAL; I had a few clients who just couldn't afford to pay my fee. But I have not offered any type of refund anticipation loan in years. I feel that the fees are unconscionable.

Although having worked at H&R Block, I understand the situation. There are taxpayers out there who need to have their tax return done, and they don't have two nickels to rub together.

If RALs were done away with, it would be a problem—there would be at least a few hundred thousand taxpayers who would have no way to get their tax return done in order to get their EIC.

Which software program do you use?

Chet: I use UltraTax. I love it. It's pricey, but it's got everything. For example, it's got the 1045 automatically calculating. I love the way it handles shareholder basis. It does a fabulous job tracking basis and transferring it over to the 1040. And it does a really good job with passive activity losses, too.

Did you use UltraTax from the start?

Chet: I did. It was a big chunk of change the first couple of years. At the beginning, I got evaluation copies of five different tax software packages. I processed three to four dummy returns and UltraTax just jumped out ahead of the pack.

So you decided to use UltraTax based on the evaluation copies. Obviously you worked for H&R Block beforehand, but they have their own proprietary software.

Chet: Yes, and it's pretty clunky. I started getting evaluation copies pretty early, while I was still studying for the EA exam. When I was studying, I would enter cases into the software programs just to see how the software handled the situation.

After my first tax season, I knew it would take a few years to build a client base. So the following autumn, I went to the Creative Solutions seminar for UltraTax.

I created an introductory letter that I handed out to everybody at the update. Basically, the letter said that I had time available for any local tax firm that had some peak season overload, that I was available to help. One of the attendees took the letter back to the managing partner of her firm.

It was a small firm with five accountants, three of whom were CPAs. I worked for them thirty hours a week for two years, until I had enough clients that I stopped doing any outsource work. I did this the second and third year I was in business. I also taught basic tax classes for Jackson Hewitt to pick up additional revenue.

Is there anything else you'd like to add?

Chet: The Georgia Association of Enrolled Agents formed a 501(c)(3)—an educational foundation that provides scholarship money to help pay for EA study materials and also to defray the cost of the EA exam. Many Enrolled Agents have benefited from our scholarship money. This is our fourth year.

It's called the GAEA Educational Foundation. The last couple of years we've given out between six and seven thousand dollars.

Aspiring EAs or even licensed EAs that want to go to NTPI (the National Tax Practice Institute) in Washington, GAEA will cover their registration fee for NTPI.

Chapter 14

Networking for Representation Referrals

"What's the difference between an IRS auditor and a Rottweiler?
A Rottweiler eventually lets go."

-Anonymous

Networking Boosts Your Profile

Most EAs belong to at least one professional organization, such as the National Association of Enrolled Agents (NAEA), or the National Association of Tax Professionals (NATP). Most of us join with the hope that we will get information about continuing education events in our area, and we might attend one or two gatherings throughout the year. Most of us are "too busy" to participate in much more than that, right?

Wrong!

All the EAs highlighted in this book are all very active in their local professional organizations. And the *more* active they are, the more *successful* they are. Why? Because successful EAs know that networking is a big part of their success. Networking is *good for business.*

This advice doesn't just include tax organizations. Don't be afraid to join other civic groups that might benefit your practice and raise your community profile.

Networking with other tax pros can be a source of valuable free advice. You can learn from other professionals how they built their tax practices. And networking can be a source of clients—you get the inside scoop whenever a tax professional is about to retire and wants to put his or her practice up for sale.

Representation Tips

Some EAs do progress billing with an *agreement* that if the client does not pay an invoice within a certain time frame, (say, thirty days) the representation will cease and the Power of Attorney will be revoked. Couple this strategy with a firmly-worded stop-work letter and even your most difficult clients will quickly understand that you *mean business.*

As many of us already know, the majority of representation clients are taxpayers who have gotten themselves into trouble. Gross errors on self-prepared returns or huge red flags from excessive deductions will often bring these frantic taxpayers into your office.

Representation is profitable, but difficult work. Dealing with the IRS is never easy. Many state taxing authorities are also difficult. You must be prepared to deal with both of them. If you decide to incorporate IRS representation and make it a big part of your practice, there are some basic rules that can help you succeed.

1. Always ask for a retainer in advance. A good rule of thumb is to estimate the amount of time the engagement will take, and ask for at least one-third of the billable hours that you expect to incur. Don't work for free.

2. Always use an engagement letter. No exceptions. Spell out everything in clear terms.

3. Get two signatures. If the taxpayer is married, insist that the spouse sign the engagement letter, too (unless it is an innocent spouse case). If you smell "something fishy" about a case, like a husband who does not want his wife to be present while you are discussing their joint tax return, consider withdrawing from the engagement. The last thing you need is a lawsuit on your hands from an angry spouse who was kept in the dark about an IRS audit.

4. Give them a firm deadline. Set a definite time frame for when you will terminate the engagement if payments are not received. Thirty days is a good number. Offer to take a credit card number and bill monthly as necessary.

5. Clearly discuss payment terms. Always go over the items in your engagement letter and have the taxpayer initial each major point. Explain the retainer. Always get a signature. You can also have a staff member do this.

Sample Engagement Letter

Dear Mr. Ramsey,

This letter is a confirmation of the financial arrangement regarding representation and consulting services that our office will be providing to you. I, John Smith, EA will be representing you, *Blake Ramsey*, before the Internal Revenue Service for the examination of your individual tax returns for tax years 2007 and 2008. I will represent you personally before the IRS and in other matters if the IRS expands the scope of their investigation.

My fees are based on an hourly rate of $225. My staff rate is currently $65 per hour. You will be charged actual cost for any ancillary costs, such as FedEx shipping or postage.

I require a retainer of $2,500. Work will not commence until after the retainer is received. Invoices will be paid against this retainer. My invoices are due upon receipt. If an invoice is not paid within 30 days of issuance, work on the engagement will cease immediately, and we will revoke our Power of Attorney with the IRS. Late fees of 1.5% per month apply on all late invoices.

Sincerely,

John Smith, EA

Client Signature: *Blake Ramsey*

Interview with Gary W. Lundgren, EA

Proactive Taxpayer Advocates
www.Taxpayer-Advocates.net

Professional Designations: Enrolled Agent, Former Revenue Officer for the State of Minnesota

So how did you become an Enrolled Agent?

Gary: I took the Enrolled Agent exam. I was previously a revenue officer for the State of Minnesota. All the state tax agencies are more aggressive than the IRS because they have better collection tools.

After you took the EA exam, did you decide right away to focus on representation?

Gary: Yes. When I worked for the state, I did joint projects with the IRS. I was involved in drafting tax legislation and I served as an expert witness in Tax Court. So I was involved at some high levels. Several IRS agents knew me. I worked in the field performing collections, investigations, and property seizures.

So when you started out, how did you obtain your representation clients?

Gary: Networking. My primary contacts are accountants and attorneys. I also network with anyone who is self-employed, such as real estate agents or small business owners. They are always good prospects.

Before the Internet became popular, most of my referrals were from attorneys or accountants. They would refer their representation cases to me. I did the dirty work that no one else wanted to do.

How did you make the connection with the other professionals?

Gary: I contacted many of the accountants and attorneys I knew when I was a revenue officer. I also networked with family and friends, and made new contacts. My practice just grew naturally. I got one referral after another; pretty soon, I had a couple hundred clients.

How quickly did your tax practice grow? Were you able to support yourself right away?

Gary: It took two years to build up. I took on a part-time job until I had enough clients to support me.

When I took a part-time job, I avoided work in retail because I didn't want my clients to see me. I took only part-time jobs where I wasn't likely to see the public. I wanted clients to see me as *successful* from the very beginning. After two years, I was able to get an office space and hired my wife as a full-time employee.

So when you get a referral, do you only take over the representation? Do you refer the client back when the audit is done?

Gary: We work as a team with the other professionals. They send the client to me. I do the representation and the other professional continues his/her work to do the accounting or tax preparation. When I get done with a client, they continue their relationship with the referring professional.

Do you do any tax preparation at all?

Gary: I do some tax preparation, just to keep my skills up. I do about fifty tax returns a year. My specialty is in compliance and collection issues. There's a lot of complexity in that alone. If a tax return is very complex, I will generally refer it out. I think that Enrolled Agents should focus on their talents that best serve the client.

So you think it's better for EAs to specialize?

Gary: Yes. It's like the world of medicine. Your podiatrist is not going to do your heart surgery.

Do you always use an engagement letter?

Gary: Yes, I always use an engagement letter, and I always get a retainer up-front. Even in the case of referrals, I always deal financially direct with the client.

Do you have any clients out-of-state?

Gary: I have more out-of-state clients than I do clients within the state. I get referrals from all sources. I got a call from a client in Santa Barbara yesterday; someone else had referred her to me.

Sometimes I don't know where the referrals come from. I've been in business for over twenty years, so the referrals are going to happen naturally. I taught some classes and seminars, and I think that some of my referrals are generated from that.

Do you use Internet advertising?

Gary: I just have a website. I designed it myself. But I don't rely on the Internet very much as a marketing tool. I still network a lot. I used to buy tax-lien lists. You can buy over the Internet these days. Tax liens are public information. You can go down to the courthouse and write down the names and addresses if you want. I used the tax-lien lists to mail out letters. I used to do 500 pieces a month. I usually got two to three clients out of a mailing. So it paid for itself. I also do an e-newsletter.

Can you explain your newsletter as a marketing tool?

Gary: Yes, it's called *eTaxNews.* I have a sign-up form on my website. I have hundreds of subscribers. I've been doing a newsletter for a few years. I write about anything that I think might be of interest to my clients. Sometimes I write just general information.

I remind people about estimated tax payments. The IRS is also a great source of news, and you can plagiarize them![35] The newsletter is a way to keep in touch with people.

Resources Section

How to Notify the IRS If You Have Moved

For Enrolled Agents who have moved since their last renewal, notify IRS by email, fax or mail OPR at:

Office of Practitioner Enrollment
P.O. Box 33968
Detroit, MI 48232, or
Fax to (313) 234-1293

The Enrolled Agent's name, prior address, new address, Social Security number or tax identification number, and the date must be included.

The IRS needs current address information in order to mail out the renewal of enrollment information.

Errors and Omissions Insurance

Placer Insurance Agency
P.O. Box 619052,
Roseville, CA 95661-9052
License# 0C66701
Direct Phone: 916-797-4420
Toll Free: 877-877-0770
WWW.TAXPROEANDO.COM

Professional Organizations

American Institute of Professional Bookkeepers

www.aipb.org

The most widely respected national bookkeeping association and certification, established in 1987. The board members are highly respected members of the financial community—this organization was founded by two Certified Public Accountants, Stanley Hartman and Stephen Sahlein.

National Association of Enrolled Agents (NAEA)

www.naea.org

The NAEA is a national association of over 11,000 independent, licensed tax professionals called Enrolled Agents (EA). They are the largest national organization dedicated just to Enrolled Agents. They offer a wide range of membership benefits including CPE and the well-known publication, *The EA Journal.* Every member automatically joins the national chapter when he or she joins a state chapter.

National Association of Tax Professionals (NATP)

www.natptax.com

The largest association of tax professionals, founded in 1979. Members include unenrolled practitioners, Enrolled Agents, accountants, CPAs, attorneys, and financial planners. NATP offers a tax resource and education center. They offer year-round CPE. NATP has a tax store that sells tax prep materials (such as folders and client newsletters).

They also offer the NATP Tax Professional Fee Study, which is a yearly fee study that's worth the price of membership alone. Find out what other preparers around the country are charging and what software they use: very good information.

National Society of Accountants (NSA)

(Formerly the NSPA)

www.nsacct.org

Originally started in 1945, NSA has a membership of 12,000. Today, the NSA continues to support the Enrolled Agent program by offering an Enrolled Agent preparatory course. In 1973, the NSA established ACAT (Accreditation Council for Accountancy and Taxation) as an independent credentialing body to provide a standard of competency in the area of public accounting.

In 1976, NSA launched the National Accounting Forum, a two-day program featuring sixteen hours of CPE. Later, to help its members provide high quality professional services, the NSA introduced the National Estate Tax conferences and the ACAT Review Course.

National Society of Tax Professionals

www.nstp.org

The NSTP was founded in 1985. Membership is open to most practicing financial professionals. The NSTP offers a wide range of membership benefits, including CPE and discounts on products.

Education and Licensing Resources

Accreditation Council for Accountancy and Taxation® (ACAT)

www.acatcredentials.org

ACAT credentials are a valuable way to raise proficiencies, earn professional recognition, gain a competitive edge, boost business and jumpstart careers. There are four designations offered:

- Accredited Business Accountant® (ABA)
- Accredited Tax Advisor® (ATA)
- Accredited Tax Preparer® (ATP)
- Elder Care Specialist™ (ECS)

A proficiency exam, experience requirement, and continuing education are required for each designation. You must also agree to adhere to a code of ethics.

QuickBooks ProAdvisor® Program

www.proadvisor.intuit.com

The QuickBooks ProAdvisor program is well respected by the general public and accounting professionals alike. Many Enrolled Agents become ProAdvisors and continue to renew their certification every year. Many EAs report that Intuit's ProAdvisor program is a constant source of referrals year after year.

Thompson Prometric

www.prometric.com

Thompson Prometric is the exclusive administrator of the IRS Enrolled Agent exam. Prometric has testing centers all over the United States. Accommodations are available for disabled students. You can find out more about the IRS EA exam by going to Prometric's website. You may schedule your appointment for the testing period May 1- February 28. There is no testing in March and April.

Universal Accounting Center

www.universalaccounting.com

The Universal Accounting Center trains accountants, tax preparers, and bookkeepers. They offer practice building, tax preparer training, and QuickBooks' courses. They offer professional designations, such as the Professional Bookkeeper (PB) and Professional Tax Preparer (PTP).

Even if you are already a tax professional, these additional designations can help raise your profile and increase your marketability.

Contributors

Owen Arnoff, EA

Better Business Ventures, Inc.

www.BetterBusinessVentures.com

A native New Yorker, Owen relocated to California in 1983. After having spent a brief period of time as a representative of Funeral Security Plans in Chico, California, he moved to Sacramento in 1984 and began a career in the insurance business, first with Mutual of Omaha Insurance Company and later as an Agency Manager for Center West Insurance Agency.

In 1996, Owen was recruited by a regional franchisee involved in the vehicle cosmetic repair business where he became the Chief Financial Officer for more than four years. Concurrently, he also founded what would become Better Business Ventures, Inc. in April 1997.

Currently, Better Business Ventures, Inc. performs a variety of financial services for individuals and small business owners. Among the services he continues to provide are tax preparation services as an Enrolled Agent and consulting as a Certified QuickBooks ProAdvisor (since 1999).

Gary W. Lundgren, EA

Proactive Taxpayer Advocates
www.Taxpayer-Advocates.net

Gary W. Lundgren, EA has over twenty-eight years of experience in general/cost accounting and tax issues.

For eight years, he was a Revenue Officer for the state of Minnesota and has been an Enrolled Agent (EA) since 1994.

Gary researches and analyzes tax regulations, resolves tax issues and disputes for individuals and businesses, and has done forensic accounting and tax evasion investigations. Intense negotiations with government agencies and clients showcase his skills in communication, analysis, tax planning, and organization. Gary has a busy tax practice in California and serves clients all over the United States.

Darrell M. Carp, EA

Carp Tax Services, Inc.
www.CarpTaxServices.com

Darrell is an Enrolled Agent and former IRS Revenue Officer. He was an IRS Section Chief, Group Manager, Assistant Branch Chief, and Regional Analyst. Darrell retired from the IRS after fifteen years of service and started his own highly successful tax practice in 1989.

His tax practice is located in Erial, New Jersey. He serves clients all over the United States.

Chet Burgess, EA

Brookwood Tax Service

www.BrookwoodTax.com

Chet is the owner of Brookwood Tax Service, LLC. Brookwood Tax Service is located in Georgia. Chet is a graduate of Washington and Lee University, and formerly worked for a large national tax preparation firm before starting his own professional tax practice.

He is a member of the National Association of Tax Professionals (NATP), the largest professional association of tax specialists in the nation. Chet also serves as the President of the Georgia Association of Enrolled Agents.

Both organizations provide frequent alerts to their members of tax law changes and IRS ruling and procedure updates, and both provide extensive continuing education programs for their members.

Kristin Delfau, EA MA

Delfau Tax & Financial Services
www.delfautax.com

A native of Pennsylvania, Kristin relocated to Connecticut in 2002 after studying and working abroad on two continents. In 2004, she joined an independent tax and financial planning firm in Brookfield, Connecticut where she became a licensed Investment Advisory Representative with Series 6, 62, 63, and 65 licenses, as well as a tax preparer and planner. She also earned her insurance licenses.

In 2007, Kristin became an Enrolled Agent, and was contracted to write *Turbo-Mom's Guide to Saving Money Without Wasting Time* (Aji, 2009). In 2008, she founded her own tax and financial planning firm, Delfau Tax & Financial Services, based on a flat-fee billing platform.

In 2009, *Turbo-Mom's Guide* was published and later that year, Kristin left the securities industry to focus on what she truly enjoyed: the tax and insurance aspects of her firm. She only works with individuals, sole proprietors, and one-owner LLCs and provides them with true tax and insurance planning year after year. Kristin is a member of NY/CT Association of Tax Professionals as well as the NATP. She is also a Fulbright scholar and speaks fluent French.

Dineen Huft

Placer Insurance Agency

Dineen M. Huft is currently licensed to transact insurance in fifty states. For the last thirty years, Dineen and her firm Placer Insurance Agency [36]has been providing professional liability insurance to Enrolled Agents, Certified Public Accountants, and other tax professionals.

Currently, Dineen and her firm insure over 2,500 tax firms throughout the United States. Dineen participates in insurance coverage design, claims, and risk management.

Dineen is an active contributor to the California Society of Enrolled Agents and the National Society of Enrolled Agents, and conducts risk management seminars for tax professionals throughout the US.

David Hatt, EA MS

www.DavidHattEA.com

David Hatt grew up in the San Francisco Bay Area. He has had many careers and found one that made him thrive and "not work a single day" (as his EA colleague, Jim Southward is fond of saying).

David Hatt is an Enrolled Agent in Menlo Park, California. He has an undergraduate degree in finance from San Diego State University and a Master's in taxation from California State University East Bay in Hayward, California.

He is the Immediate Past President of NAEA, a member of the California Society of Enrolled Agents and a member of Mission Society (CA) of Enrolled Agents. He is also a Graduate Fellow of NTPI.

Gabrielle Fontaine, PB

www.TheFreelanceBookkeeper.com

Gabrielle Fontaine, PB is a freelance Professional Bookkeeper and Advanced Certified QuickBooks ProAdvisor who assists Internet savvy entrepreneurs and self-employed professionals to get their books under control, save taxes, and maximize profits. Her primary business website is *www.BookkeepingDirect.com.*

For over twenty-seven years, Gabrielle has worked in finance and administration, offering her services in a freelance capacity for the last twenty years. Specifically, Gabrielle specializes in QuickBooks consulting and training, assisting her clients on a virtual basis, exclusively via the telephone and Internet.

She is a nationally published writer both online and offline of business articles, reports, and an industry-specific business operations manual. She is the co-author of *How to Start a Successful Home-Based Freelance Bookkeeping and Tax Preparation Business.* Gabrielle currently publishes her popular free online newsletter at *www.TheFreelanceBookkeeper.com*

Bill Fulcher, EA MBA

www.billfulcher.com

William Lester (Bill) Fulcher, Jr. worked a year as an organizer for Teamster's Local 657 in San Antonio. He and his ex-wife Shirley Sanderson, a professional bookkeeper, started their business together in 1968 after taking courses in accounting and taxes.

Bill obtained a Bachelor of Business Administration degree from Pan American University, with a major in accounting in 1979 and a Master of Business Administration (MBA) degree in 1983.

Bill is a life member of the Texas Association of Financial and Tax Specialists; a member of the National and Texas Associations of Enrolled Agents; and a member of the National Lawyers' Guild and its local chapter.

A prolific writer, Bill has contributed many articles to the National Public Accountant; he also wrote a weekly financial column for the Brownsville Herald for nine years and still contributes an occasional article for that local daily newspaper on politics, tax, and finance.

About The Author

Christy Pinheiro, EA ABA®

Christy Pinheiro is an Enrolled Agent, Accredited Business Advisor®, and financial writer. She is the author of multiple books on taxation, bookkeeping, and management. Her finance and tax articles have been nationally published online and in various periodicals. She is a proud member of the National Association of Tax Professionals and the National Association of Enrolled Agents.

Among Christy's books is a complete study guide series for the IRS Enrolled Agent Exam. Her personal website is *www.ChristyPinheiro.com.*

Her publishing company is PassKey Publications at *www.PassKeyPublications.com.*

Index

A

B

C

D

E

F

S

T

U

Endnotes

[1] OIC- IRS Offers in Compromise: An offer in compromise (OIC) is an agreement between a taxpayer and the IRS that settles the taxpayer's tax liabilities for less than what they owe.
[2] Edwards, Paul and Sarah. The Best Home Businesses for the 90s.
[3] www.Payscale.com, www.EHow.com.
[4] NATP fee study, 2008.
[5] National Association of Tax Professionals. NATP 2008 fee study.
[6] All You Need To Know About the IRS. Strassels, Paul.
[7] David C. Johnston , 2005. Perfectly Legal: The Covert Campaign to Rig Our Tax System to Benefit the Super-Rich-And Cheat-Everybody- Else.
[8] Transactional Records Access Clearinghouse (TRAC), Syracuse University.
[9] *www.universalaccounting.com.*
[10] *How to Make it Big as a Consultant.* Cohen, William.
[11] US Department of Justice. Case Docket# 2:09-cr-120-MCE. U.S. Attorney Lawrence G. Brown, 3/17/2009.
[12] NATP TAXPro Journal. Summer 2009. *Sorting Out Software.*
[13] IR-2007-91.
[14] Adobe Acrobat help pages.
[15] IRS Revenue Ruling 97-22.
[16] Small Business Taxes and Management. Daily Update, Dec 15th, 2000. IRS loses client files.
[17] NATP, National Association of Tax Professionals. 2008 Fee Study.
[18] Barnett, Gary. Death and Taxes. *www.lewrockwell.com*
[19] Name has been changed.
[20] According to Placer Insurance Agency.
[21] *www.taxproeando.com.* Placer Insurance Agency.
[22] Placer Insurance Agency. Enrolled Agent Professional Liability Coverage.
[23] Information provided by Placer Insurance Agency.
[24] Bureau of Labor Statistics. *www.bls.gov*
[25] NATP 2008 Fee Study.
[26] Tax preparer survey done by the author.
[27] http://en.wikipedia.org/wiki/Nonassurance_services.
[28] *www.Indeed.com.*
[29] A "wet signature" is an original signature on a piece of paper, rather than an electronic signature (over the Internet) or a faxed/photocopied signature. Many states still require a wet signature for certain insurance or legal transactions.

[30] Name has been changed.
[31] The IRS EA exam used to be a four-part written exam. The EA exam is now a three-part computerized exam administered exclusively by Thompson Prometric.
[32] www.bni.com
[33] Voice Over Internet Protocol (VoIP) is a technology that allows users to place calls over the Internet, using IP lines, rather than phone lines. Costs are traditionally much cheaper.
[34] www.climark.com.
[35] IRS regulations and publications are public domain and not subject to copyright.
[36] Premier Agency, Inc. dba Placer Insurance Agency.

www.ingramcontent.com/pod-product-compliance
Lightning Source LLC
LaVergne TN
LVHW050617100826
845148LV00011B/1627

* 9 7 8 0 9 8 2 2 6 6 0 4 5 *